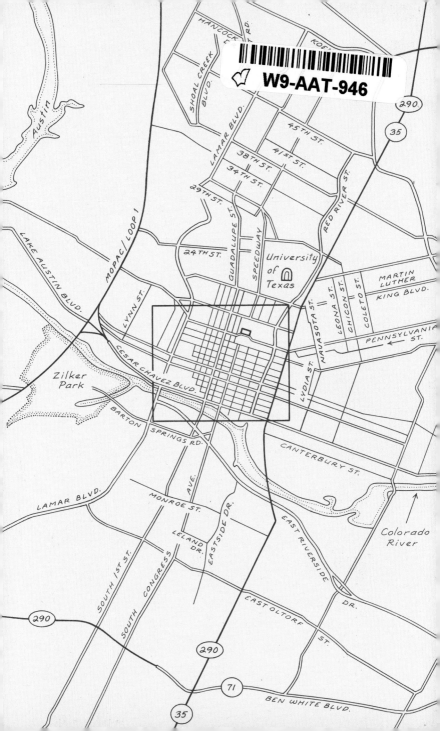

# The Great Psychedelic Armadillo Picnic

## A "Walk" in Austin

*Kinky Friedman*

CROWN JOURNEYS

CROWN PUBLISHERS · NEW YORK

*Published by Crown Journeys, an imprint of Crown Publishers, New York,
New York.*
*Member of the Crown Publishing Group, a division of Random House, Inc.*
*www.crownpublishing.com*

*CROWN JOURNEYS and the Crown Journeys colophon are trademarks
of Random House, Inc.*

*Portions previously appeared in* Texas Monthly.

*Printed in the United States of America*

*Design by Lauren Dong*
*Map by Jackie Aher*

*Library of Congress Cataloging-in-Publication Data*
*Friedman, Kinky.*
   *The great psychedelic armadillo picnic : a "walk" in Austin / Kinky
Friedman.—1st ed.*
      *p. cm.*
   *1. Austin (Tex.)—Guidebooks. 2. Austin (Tex.)—Social life and customs.
3. Austin (Tex.)—Biography. 4. Celebrities—Texas—Austin—Biography.
I. Title.*
   *F394.A93F75   2004*
   *917.64'310464—dc22*

                                                         *2004013161*

*ISBN 1-4000-5070-7*

*10   9   8   7   6   5   4   3   2   1*

*First Edition*

*Dedicated to all the people over the past forty years*
*who told me I couldn't write this masterpiece.*

# CONTENTS

*The* *Great Psychedelic*
*Armadillo Picnic*

## Introduction

Time, they say, changes the river. Time changes the city, too. Over the years, many people have helped Austin to shine in the spotlight, bask in the limelight, and skinny-dip in the moonlight. There's Mirabeau B. Lamar, Sam Houston, and Stephen F. Austin. There's J. Frank Dobie, John Henry Faulk, and Doug Sahm. There's Liz Carpenter, Molly Ivins, and Ann Richards. There's George W., Lance Armstrong, and Barbara Jordan. Then there's the next governor of the state, yours truly, Kinky Friedman (if I'm elected the first Jewish governor of Texas, I'll reduce the speed limits to $54.95!).

Austin is a city nurtured by generations of musicians, politicians, and beauticians. With her countless clubs, bars, and dance halls, Austin is a whore with a heart of gold flaunting her gaudy neon necklace in the Texas night. In Austin they say when you die, you go to Willie Nelson's house. I can't swear this is true but I do know if you come here you'll find that the music is great, the beer is cold, and the natives are friendly. If you're lucky enough to hang around awhile, you'll discover for yourself that the spirit of Austin is a puff of Willie, a riff of Stevie Ray, and a little piece of Janis's heart.

# The Barenaked Essentials

L IKE MOST OTHER BUSY CITIES THESE DAYS, AUSTIN is not very effectively traversed by foot. Indeed, if you're crazy enough to try, you might very well find yourself getting T-boned by a shuttle bus. There *are* places you can walk, jog, loiter, or hop around angrily in a circle, and we will get to these momentarily. But you must understand that "a walk in Austin" is primarily a spiritual sort of thing. You're going to need a four-wheeled penis of some kind. If you want to fit in perfectly, I'd recommend a pickup truck with a "God Bless John Wayne" bumper sticker.

As long as we're on the subject, what, exactly *is* Austin? If you were to round up a flock of random Austinites from around the city and present them with that question, you would get such answers as "home of the University of Texas"; "the live music capital of the world"; "birthplace of Dell Computers." Oddly enough, it is unlikely that any of those Austinites would say that Austin is the capital of Texas, or that Austin used to be a settlement named Waterloo, or that a man with the unlikely name of Mirabeau B. Lamar led the fight to make Austin the Capital of the Republic of Texas over Waco and Houston. See, we Austinites don't know enough about the background of our fair city, but you, dear visitor, will not be so impaired. Read on for the barenaked essentials of Austin, intended to give you a bit of background on the town O. Henry nicknamed "The Violet Crown."

ONCE UPON A TIME, when relations between cowboys and Indians were only slightly better than the level of violence in a modern American city, a man drank an entire bottle of mescal, ate the worm at the bottom, and got so high he needed a stepladder to scratch his ass. The man was named Mirabeau B. Lamar. The year was 1836. It was a good year for mescal. It was also a good year for Austin, in spite of the fact that it wasn't there yet.

Texas had just won her independence from Mexico. Eighty-four years later the future first female governor of Texas, "Ma" Ferguson, would say, "If English was good enough for Jesus Christ, it's good enough for Texas!"

The new nation was christened the Republic of Texas, and with open arms she welcomed settlers to her ample bosom. In an area roughly located at the nipple of this bosom, a camp town named Waterloo grew. Among

Waterloo's new citizens was former Georgian Mirabeau B. Lamar. Despite being from Georgia, Lamar was a true renaissance man who excelled at horseback riding and fencing, wrote poetry, painted in oils, read voraciously, and collected matchbooks from many restaurants. He became a senator for Georgia by the time he was thirty-one, and his career in Georgia politics looked promising until his wife, Tabitha, stricken with tuberculosis, was bugled to Jesus in 1830. Mirabeau was devastated by her death, and like any poet worth his iambic pentameter, he used his grief to write several of his best-known poems (among them *An Evening on the Banks of the Chattahoochie* and *Thou Idol of My Soul*). In the meantime his political career stagnated. Lamar's friend James Fannin had a home in the new Republic of Texas, and he invited Lamar to visit in hopes the trip would lift his pal out of despair.

Like a lot of people who visit Texas, Mirabeau fell in love with the state and decided to stay. He was in Georgia preparing for his move to Texas when he heard about the massacres at the Alamo, during which Davy Crockett and Jim Bowie were killed, and at Goliad, where his friend Fannin and 341 other Texas freedom fighters were taken prisoner and ordered executed by General Santa Anna.

The news spurred Lamar to immediately cut buns back to Texas to join the revolution as a private. He was soon commissioned a colonel on the field of San Jacinto just before the famous battle. The gentleman poet distinguished himself as a soldier on the battlefield by his bravery and quick actions. Texas came away from the battle victorious, and so did Lamar. With his political career back on track, he was made Secretary of War in the cabinet of *ad interim* President David G. Burnet. In the fall of 1836, in the Republic's first presidential election, Lamar became the vice-president of Texas. Sam Houston, a major general who led Lamar and other soldiers to victory at the Battle of San Jacinto, was elected president.

Sam Houston was one of the great characters in Austin's history. As an adolescent he ran away from home to live among the Cherokees, who adopted him and gave him the Indian name *Colonneh,* or "Raven." Young Sam viewed the chief of the band, Oolooteka, as his Indian father, and the tribe much as a surrogate family. He found peace living *la vida* Indian and he enjoyed it for several years before he decided it was time to hang up his toma-hawk and strike out on his own.

The inner peace Houston found with the Cherokees was quickly sucked dry by the white man's world. In 1829, after a failed marriage and the subsequent nosedive of his political aspirations due to rumors of his infidelity and alcoholism, Houston returned to Chief Oolooteka's band and stayed for three years. He tried to revisit the tranquil-lity he had enjoyed with the tribe in his youth, but he drank so heavily that he allegedly received the nickname "Big Drunk." Somewhere between drinking and brawl-ing, Houston married a Cherokee woman from the tribe (Tiana Rogers, a distant relative of Will Rogers) and worked as a commercial agent for his adopted clan. While Sam was on official business in Washington, an unfortunate congressman accused him of corruption and Houston rebutted the charge by whupping the accuser's ass right there on the street. The ensuing public trial put Houston back at center stage, a move he later said gave him back his will to live. He was found guilty for contempt of Congress and given a five-hundred-dollar fine. Houston's former commander during the War of 1812, Andrew Jackson, now the U.S. president, paid Houston's fine on his last day in office.

By 1836 the brawling, womanizing, alcoholic Sam Houston rode the wave of popularity as "Old Sam Jacinto" (for his successful defeat of Santa Anna's army at the battle of San Jacinto) and served as president of Texas for two terms.

In 1838, after Houston's final term in office, Lamar decided to run for president. He won the office after the other two candidates both committed suicide before election day. It was this renaissance man from Georgia who began to champion the fledgling settlement of Waterloo to be the official capital of Texas.

President Lamar inherited a Texas that had no money, no commercial treaties, no international recognition (except from the U.S.), and no chance of annexation by the United States. Texas was under constant Indian attack, and Mexico continued to be a threat. Lamar, however, was a romantic. He envisioned a Texas whose borders

would reach the Pacific Ocean. He wanted Waterloo to be the new capital, and he wanted it named after Stephen F. Austin, the man considered the founder of Anglo-American Texas.

Austin had died in service as secretary of state in 1836 at the age of forty-three. He is remembered in Texas history for his many contributions to the state, which included carrying out his father Moses' plans to establish an American colony in the Mexican province of Tejas. Stephen Austin's skillful diplomacy averted aggression from Mexico, who resented American presence on its soil. Rather than call upon his settlers to take up arms against Mexico, Austin believed there was still a chance to persuade the government peacefully to allow his colony to stay. He traveled all the way to Mexico City to secure a new law confirming his right to colonize his father's land. A large number of settlers from the United States moved south to join his new colony. Austin's unassuming presence and kindly manner were deeply respected by even the most unruly colonists in the settlement. For his tireless efforts on behalf of Texas, it was fitting that Austin be given the honor of having the capital of Texas named for him.

In addition to making Waterloo the capital of the new republic, Lamar also wanted to establish a system of education that would be funded by the state's ample wealth in land. He passionately believed in a strong education system for all the citizens of Texas; he would later be remembered in history as "the Father of Texas Education."

Sam Houston felt that Waterloo was too far from the coast and too close to Mexico to be the capital of the Republic of Texas. He felt that the city of Houston would be a better placement strategically, but Lamar prevailed and Waterloo, by then called Austin, temporarily became the capital in 1839.

The entire government of the Republic of Texas arrived from the city of Houston in oxcarts to set up shop in Austin. Edwin Waller, the future first mayor of Austin, was hired to lay out the street plan for the city, and it remains mostly intact today from First Street to 15th Street downtown. The struggle to make Austin the permanent capital of Texas lasted for thirty years; in 1872, Austin finally won out over the cities of Houston and Waco by popular vote to become the official capital of the twenty-eighth state of the Union. In later years, Austin's population boomed. Because of the new Houston and Texas Central Railway, Austin became a huge trading center. An international population of newcomers made the city their home, creating the diversity that still exists today. Lamar's dream of a solid education system was realized by 1881, when Austin was chosen as the site for the new University of Texas (see "Austin Landmarks"). That same year the public school system was started. Austin was well on her way to becoming the city whose personality nurtured the likes of O. Henry, Janis Joplin, Michael Dell, and, of course, myself.

Now, as we creep into the twenty-first century, Austin

has grown to a population of roughly 657,000. It is the fourth-largest city in Texas and the sixteenth-largest city in the United States. Austin serves as the seat of Travis county (named after one of the defenders of the Alamo, William B. Travis). The University of Texas at Austin is the flagship campus of the vast University of Texas system. Other institutes of higher learning include Austin Community College (called ACC), Concordia University, Houston-Tillotson College (founded in 1881), and St. Edward's University (founded in 1885). Austin has a hearty mix of educators, students, politicians, and lobby-ists, as well as techno-geeks, actors, musicians, rascals, and transients. It is the self-proclaimed "live music capital of the world." The city's biggest employers, should you decide to extend your visit permanently, include the State of Texas, UT-Austin, Dell Computer, Motorola, IBM, and high-tech giant National Instruments. Austin is the home to several well-known directors such as Mike Judge *(King of the Hill)*, Robert Rodriguez *(Once Upon a Time in Mexico)*, Richard Linklater *(Slacker)* and Tobe Hooper *(The Texas Chainsaw Massacre)*. The city hosts the annual Texas Book Festival as well as South by Southwest, which has become our own little Sundance, attracting films of all types from around the world.

Present-day Austin is situated on the Colorado River, with three lakes within the city limits: Town Lake, Lake Austin, and Lake Travis. We are also on top of the Balcones Fault (upon which we not so wisely placed IH-35). The geography of the city is varied. The eastern part of Austin is flat while the western part is scenic rolling hills. The main sector of Austin, simply called "Downtown" by locals, is about ten miles tall and three miles wide. The main north-south thoroughfares are Mopac/Loop 1; Lamar Blvd.; South First/Guadalupe; South Congress/Speedway; and IH-35.

The main east-west thoroughfares are Koenig/290; 45th Street; 38th Street; Martin Luther King (MLK); Cesar Chavez; Oltorf; and Ben White (called 360 west of Mopac and Highway 71 east of IH-35). Any street preceded by "North" (as in North Lamar) is north of the Colorado River. Any street preceded by "South" (S. Congress) is south of the river. Austin streets have the alarming habit of abruptly changing names as you are driving down them. For example, Speedway becomes Congress south of MLK; Guadalupe becomes S. First south of the river; Mopac is also called Loop 1; and Koenig is also called Highway 290. The last thing you need to know about downtown streets is that most of them are one-way, except Congress. Even-numbered streets are westbound (like Sixth Street) and odd-numbered streets are eastbound (like Fifth Street). Guadalupe is two-way for most of the way except deep downtown between MLK and Cesar Chavez (where it is southbound only). Any good map of Austin will clear it up. Go get one.

Austin's neighborhoods are divided by the locals into the following:

CENTRAL AUSTIN, OR DOWNTOWN. This houses the Central Business District, the Capital Complex, the Entertainment District, and the University of Texas. Among the students, politicians, professors, transients, and business-droids you will find just about whatever you can imagine as far as hairstyle, clothing, body art, and pocket change go. You can come here to either stand out or blend in, whatever your pleasure may be.

EAST AUSTIN. This area used to be the scary place where nice people didn't venture; some parts of East Austin are still like that, but for ethnic diversity, these neighborhoods east of IH-35 can't be beat.

WEST AUSTIN. West of downtown to Lake Travis, these neighborhoods range from student rentals to some of the city's most exclusive gated communities.

NORTH AUSTIN. Many of Austin's new apartment complexes are located here. It used to be the boomtown area, but growth has been more northwest lately.

NORTHWEST AUSTIN. One of Austin's fastest-growing sectors. Features a lot of traffic, shopping, and tedium.

Needless to say, I avoid it (but that's hard to do because I live there).

SOUTH AUSTIN. The part of town people who don't live here love the most. Sometimes it's called "the real Austin." South Congress (or SOCO, but you will never hear me saying that), Shopping District, and older neighborhoods like Travis Heights and Zilker are located in this area. The legendary Continental Club is here, too.

An interesting historical sidenote here is that after the Civil War, Austin had a neighborhood area that was known as the "Freedman Towns" where former slaves freed during the Civil War settled. They were the communities of Clarksville, from West Lynn to the railroad tracks and from 10th to Waterson; Wheatville, bounded by Rio Grande and Shoal Creek on the east and west, and by 24th and 26th on the north and south; Masontown, covering the area between Third and Sixth and Chicon and Waller; and Kincheonville, in what is now southwest Austin.

Now you have the barenaked essentials of Austin. I encourage you to grab your map, put on your boogie shoes, and step boldly out the door. The city awaits.

# Austin for Dummies

ALL MY ADULT LIFE I'VE BEEN IN THE HABIT OF giving advice to people who are happier than I am. Like most born-again Texans, I'm sure you're thrilled right now about visiting here. Oh, you've no doubt heard stories about the wide-open spaces being mostly between people's ears, but you didn't believe them. Now, the prospect of vacationing in Austin may make you happier than 95 percent of all dentists in America, but that doesn't mean you're going to fit in. Remember, happiness, like Texas, is a highly transitory state. So my first advice to you is the same admonition I shout every time I pass a wedding in progress: "Stop before it's too late!"

But maybe you've really set your ears back, and you're hell-bent on spending your furlough in Austin. In that case, the least you can do is follow these few simple rules of the road for all modern Bubbas and Bubbettes. This, my fine-feathered foreign friend, is friendly advice, freely given. Follow it—or get the death penalty.

1. Get you some brontosaurus-foreskin boots and a big ol' cowboy hat. Always remember, only two kinds of people can get away with wearing their hats indoors: cowboys and Jews. Try to be one of them.

2. Get your hair fixed right. If you're male, cut it into a "mullet" (short on the sides and top, long in the back—think Billy Ray Cyrus). Or you can leave it long on top and cut it short on the sides and back. When you take off your cowboy hat, you'll have what I like to refer to as the Lyle Lovett Starter Kit. If you're female, make it as big as possible, with lots of teasing and hair spray. If you can hide a Buck knife in there, you're ready. Grooming tip: If you can't find curlers big enough, use empty Dr. Pepper cans.

3. Don't make the most common mistake all non-Texans make when they come down here—confusing Amarillo with the armadillo. Amarillo is a town in the Panhandle full of people who don't like being mistaken for armadillos. They're very conservative politically. The armadillo is a gentle creature. It tends to be much more middle-of-the-road.

4. Buy you a big ol' pickup truck or a Cadillac. I myself drive a Yom Kippur Clipper. That's a Jewish Cadillac—stops on a dime and picks it up.

5. Just because you can drive on snow and ice where you come from does not mean you can drive in an Austin downpour. When it rains hard, stay home. If you have to drive, get on IH-35, move into the fast lane, and go no faster than thirty-five miles per hour. If you have to drive at night, watch out for the deer, even within the city limits. Only hit the ones with huge antlers because they make the best wall hangings. Christmas gift tip: Make you a nice fur coat with antlers and give it to your mother-in-law.

6. Remember: "Y'all" is singular, "all y'all" is plural, and "all y'all's" is plural possessive.

7. Austinites have a strange way of talking. Get used to it. In my experience, I've always heard the word "Jewish" pronounced with only one syllable, such as, "He's Juush." When they pronounce the word "Jew," of course, it's invariably with about eleven syllables. An example of this would be: "She married a Jeeeeeeewwwwww!"

8. Don't call it "soda" or "pop." It's all Coke unless it's Dr. Pepper.

9. Don't pet the dog standing in the back of the pickup, no matter how small or how cute. All truck dogs are dangerous weapons. But a dog that is not in the back of a pickup is another story. We Texans love our dogs. Like we

always say: "Money may buy you a fine dog, but only love can make it wag its tail."

10. It is now legal to carry a concealed weapon in Texas, and this includes within the Austin City limits. As a result, crime has gone down. An unfortunate side-effect, however, is that there are now about 18 million ambulatory time bombs anyplace you go, just waiting for Dustin Hoffman to pound on the hood and shout, "I'm walkin' here!" As for myself, I don't carry a weapon. If anybody wants to kill me, he's going to have to remember to bring his own gun.

11. Everything goes better with picante sauce. No exceptions.

12. Be sure you have a favorite football team. Be sure it is the Texas Longhorns.

13. Don't tell us how you did it up there. Nobody cares.

14. Practice saying that you're going to Austin for vacation rather than Texas. Austinites know there's a difference.

# And the Band Played On, and On, and On . . .

S O WHAT IS IT ABOUT AUSTIN AND ITS OBSESSION with music, you might ask. Well, I'll tell you. Music is the pulse of the city financially, culturally, and spiritually. We have it all here. Jazz, roots, country, folk, blues, rock, punk, reggae, Latin, soul. Hell, we have musicians here who can't be confined to one Zip code. Likewise, you can't capture Austin in one book, or one song, or one lifetime. The best you can do is to experience it. Here are some suggestions for where to start.

Sixth Street in downtown Austin is perhaps the street best known outside the city limits. A bird's-eye view of the entertainment district would show you a rectangle bordered by East Seventh Street in the north, Congress Avenue on the west, East Fifth on the south, and IH-35 on the east. E. 6th St. bisects the rectangle. Notice the written distinction of the number: 6th St. refers to the thing you drive or walk down; Sixth Street refers to the thing you drink or crawl down. Got it?

Sixth Street is the heartbeat of our local live music scene, with its plethora of clubs and bars. Tattoo parlors, casual cafés, fancy restaurants, and the haunted Driskill Hotel (see "Austin Landmarks") are interspersed with the watering holes. Before the suds kick your eyeballs into the gutter, take a look around at the historic buildings along E. 6th that date back to the 1800s, when it was called Pecan Street. Sixth Street even has a creek (Waller Creek) that passes through the tree-lined 700 block just off the highway.

I hope you're in the mood for music, because there's a sound for every taste: blues, jazz, country, rock, hip-hop, world, and derivations of these and other genres. You can come hungry, too, since the eats are as varied as the sounds. Chili, ribs, Tex-Mex, steak, seafood, and deli coexist next to vegetarian, Indian, Asian, Cajun, and kosher. For dessert, try some fish ice cream. Whatever cuisine you crave, Sixth Street can satisfy.

As you may have guessed, Sixth Street is frequented by the young and trendy. Fortunately for the rest of us, Sixth Street is also frequented by the old and the out of date (we prefer to call them retro), the rich and the famous, the exciting and the boring, the heroes and the scoundrels. You could find yourself pissing next to a Hollywood star, a rising politician, America's Most Wanted, or my future ex-wife. Be ready for anything.

Don't feel left out if night life ain't your thang. Sixth Street is also about fairs, festivals, and anything else that allows the gregarious city to take to the street and socialize. A Victorian Christmas on Sixth Street and the Old Pecan Street Spring Arts and Fall Arts Festival are annual arts-and-crafts shows during which the city closes off the street from IH-35 to Brazos. Vendors line the middle of Sixth in booths that sometimes spill over onto the side streets.

Don't feel roped in by the confines of Sixth Street; you're free to explore the western part of 6th, too. West 6th St. is more daytime-oriented with its antique stores, art galleries, restaurants, and eclectic shops. This area, beginning at Lamar Boulevard, includes Treaty Oak (see "Austin Landmarks"). Whole Foods, Waterloo Ice House, Amy's Ice Creams, and Sweetish Hill Bakery are some of the west side's culinary attractions. (Has it become apparent that Austin likes to eat?) The pointy-headed city planners call this end of 6th St. "the Shopping District."

Monday nights I recommend you head down to Mother Egan's Irish Pub between the hours of ten and midnight to catch the Seth Walker Band. He has a bluesy, swinging, Southern sound, and if that's not fulfilling enough, just wait; any number of local legendary musicians may show up to sit in on a number or two. Mother Egan's is located on the west end of 6th St. The Guinness is flowing, the decor is authentically Irish, and the crowd is a jolly lot (Guinness, of course, is the drink that kept the Irish from taking over the world).

Tuesday nights you can catch the happy-hour show with Toni Price at the Continental Club. Show up at six to guarantee getting your brontosaurus-foreskin boot in the door because Toni really packs the place. If you don't believe me, just drive by the club any Tuesday evening around seven, and the line filing down Congress Avenue will be too long to snort. The Continental Club is located at 1315 South Congress. The place itself is an Austin institution, and rightfully claims the title of grandfather of all local music venues because it has been here since 1957, when Morin Scott opened the establishment as a private supper club that featured touring groups like Tommy Dorsey and Glenn Miller. The Continental is believed to have been the first place in Travis County to sell liquor by the drink. In the 1960s it became a burlesque club; in the late seventies my good friends Roger "One Knite," Roddy, and Summerdog took over the club and began booking future legends like Stevie Ray Vaughan, Doug Sahm, Joe Ely, Charlie and Will Sexton, Steve Fromholtz, Greezy Wheels, The Butthole Surfers, Lee Roy Parnell, and a small but wiry band called Kinky Friedman and the Texas Jewboys.

In 1987, Steve Wertheimer took the helm and redecorated the Continental to reflect the way it looked in the fifties. Wertheimer shifted the focus of the club to the best of retro roots, rockabilly, country and swing. Happy hours here are legendary, and annual events include birthday parties for Hank Williams, Elvis, Buck Owens, and Wanda Jackson, the Queen of Rockabilly. If you're around on Monday night, don't miss the great Jane Bond.

If country is your thing, the Broken Spoke is your place. It's a true Texas honky-tonk, a south Austin icon since its inception in 1964. The Spoke, as it's affectionately called, is known for its low ceilings, friends in low places, wood-planked floor, and chicken-fried steak; my friend George W. proclaims it his favorite night spot in Austin. In fact, a picture of the then-governor Bush hangs on the wall along with photos of folks like Dwight Yoakam and Clint Eastwood. The president's picture is signed, "Thanks for the good times," and George is shown posing with the owners, James and Annetta White.

In a memorabilia room dubbed "The Tourist Trap," two-steppers can take a break by checking out Johnny Bush's boots, Bob Wills's beer can, and a chicken-fried-steak plate signed by Randy Travis. My picture hangs in there somewhere, and it's reported that upon seeing it, visitors stop dead in their tracks and openly wonder when and why in the hell Lionel Ritchie played the joint.

The Spoke has hosted country legends of the caliber of Bob Wills, Ernest Tubb, Willie Nelson, Dolly Parton, and a very young George Strait. The Whites also book local legends like the Geezinslaws, Don Walser, Alvin Crow, and the Derailers. The Spoke is a legend in itself; it has appeared in *Entertainment Weekly* and *National Geographic* as an honest representation of a by-God Texas honky-tonk.

Says James White, "On my tombstone I told my wife to just put, 'He provided a place where people could have a good time, and when he got it built, he named it the 'Broken Spoke.'" People still have a good time here, and it's probably one of the last joints you can ever go to and order a pitcher of Pearl beer.

If blues is your groove, you can't miss spending an evening at our premier blues club, Antone's. Antone's has always been synonymous with the blues, and before I go any further, let me note that Antone's is pronounced "*ÁN*-tone's," not "*ÁN*-twan's," as my pal Billy Bob Thornton always says.

Buddy Guy, Etta James, Fats Domino, Albert King, Edgar Winter, Angela Strehli, and Stevie Ray Vaughan have all graced Antone's stage. Keith Richards drops by whenever he's in town. I even darkened Antone's doors several times; I vaguely remember spending a few hours in the club because I was doing a gig, although I very well could have been there by mistake. Either way, Antone's is probably one of the main reasons Austin has such a strong blues community, and why the genre has thrived here.

Antone's was birthed during the summer of 1975 on Sixth Street and Brazos. Zydeco god Clifford Chenier busted it open, and from day one its owner, Clifford

Antone, brought in names like Muddy Waters, Willie Dixon, and Jimmy Reed for up to five-night stands. Antone also booked local blues bands like the Fabulous Thunderbirds, W.C. Clark, and Lou Ann Barton. T-Birds guitarist Jimmie Vaughan's little brother spent hours upon hours playing on stage at Antone's before he hit the big time and became one of the biggest of the modern-day blues stars. He was Stevie Ray Vaughan, Austin's hometown boy whose death is still mourned in the city.

Today, Antone's continues the tradition of live blues music. The place has survived several moves, but it is back downtown where it belongs, on Fifth and Lavaca, still playing the blues, and still serving as home away from home for the best bluesmen and blueswomen.

Other clubs you should add to your itinerary are Stubb's, Club de Ville, Joe's Generic Bar, Love Joy's, the Crown and Anchor, the Dog and Duck Pub, and Momo's. Most of the old Austin clubs that began on Sixth Street have been taken over by yuppie bars and glitzy lounges. There's even a Hard Rock Café in the heart of Sixth Street now. See you there! (Just kidding.)

Many Austinites hang out at Ninth and Red River, also known as the Red River District. It's a block of about six or seven bars. Stubbs, the largest on the strip, has an outside amphitheater where the likes of Willie Nelson and Lucinda Williams play. They have an inside club as well, with a restaurant where you can get your choppers on some of the finest barbecue in the world. The Red Eyed

Fly is devoted to rock and rockabilly, with popular bands like Echoset and Damesviolet headlining weekend shows. Headhunters is Austin's only true tiki bar, and they have island concoctions that will send your penis to Venus. Room 710 is a favorite gig spot for Hank Williams III, and Club de Ville has a great outdoor patio built into a cliff. This is one of the few areas in Austin where you are likely to run into as many native Austinites as Californians. The city council is currently trying to get a protection agency together to keep this sliver of Austin intact.

Another Austin landmark and pioneer of the Austin music scene is Threadgill's Tavern, founded by Kenneth Threadgill.

Threadgill moved to Austin in 1923. The teenaged Threadgill heard the music of his future mentor and idol Jimmie Rodgers, "the father of country music," while attending Austin High School. Subsequently, he met the legend when Threadgill worked at the Tivoli Theater in Beaumont, Texas. Backstage, Rodgers heard Threadgill imitating his yodeling and was impressed. Threadgill became a country singer later in life, and incorporated yodeling into his act; the fans loved it.

In 1933, the year Prohibition was repealed, Kenneth Threadgill moved back to Austin, where he bought an old gas station on North Lamar Boulevard. He changed the gas station into Threadgill's Tavern, which still sold gas and food but had the first beer license in Austin after the Eighteenth Amendment bit the dust. In those days, if an establishment allowed its patrons to drink and dance, it would have to pay an extra tax, so Threadgill did not allow dancing in his tavern. He and his wife Mildred ran the place until World War II, when they decided to close for a few years. During the war, Threadgill worked as a welder for the war effort, but he still kept singing here and there; in fact, Hank Williams came through Austin, and when he was late for his show at the Dessau Dance Hall, Threadgill was asked to sing a few Hank Williams songs while the audience waited. As Hank walked in, Threadgill was belting out "Lovesick Blues."

After the war, Threadgill reopened the tavern. The establishment still seated only about forty-five; it was packed on weekends when Threadgill and his Hootenanny Hoots played, and Wednesday nights became the time when cowboys, college kids, hippies, and normal Joes (increasingly rare in Austin) got together to drink beer, listen to country music, and watch Threadgill dance his trademark shuffle.

Fate guided two members of Threadgill's Hootenanny Hoots to investigate a small band of hippies they saw on the side of the road during a casual drive through Austin. Hippies were not so rare in Austin that they would warrant extra interest, but these particular longhairs had musical instruments with them, so Julie and Chuck Joyce pulled over and invited them to come to Threadgill's. The shows at the tavern were usually open-mike style, so Janis Joplin, one of the roadside hippies, stepped up that night and sang "Silver Thread and Golden Needles." When he first heard Janis sing, Threadgill was reported to have said, "That girl's really good."

Kenneth and Mildred befriended the strange young woman with the matted hair and dirty clothes. Janis became the star attraction at Threadgill's on Wednesday nights, packing in the oddly mixed crowd who came to take in the excitement swirling around her. She had yet to develop her own style, but her range and power were evident, and everyone knew she was going somewhere. Threadgill's considered her one of their own kids. After her death, Threadgill sighed, "I thought the world of that girl. I loved her."

Janis always considered Threadgill's Tavern her home; after she became famous, Kenneth always maintained that she did not get her start at Threadgill's, but rather started herself. Janis loved Kenneth Threadgill, too. In an interview she said, "He was old, a great big man with a beer belly, and white hair combed back on top of his head. He'd be dishing out Polish sausages, hard-boiled eggs, Grand Prizes, and Lonestars. Every Wednesday night, after some coaxing, Mr. Threadgill, as the students called him, would sing Jimmie Rodgers's 'T for Texas' or 'Waitin' for a Train.' Someone would say, 'Mr. Threadgill, Mr. Threadgill, come out and do us a tune.' And he'd say, 'No, I don't think so,' and they'd say, 'Come on, come on,' and he'd say, 'All right.' He'd close the bar down, and then he'd walk out the front, and he'd lay his hands on his big fat belly, which was covered with a bar apron. He'd come out like that and lean his head back and sing, just like a bird. God, was he fantastic!"

In 1970, a birthday celebration for Threadgill's was held in Oak Hill. Fans guzzled beer, ate barbecue, and enjoyed a day of music and fun. Janis was in from Hawaii. When she learned of the celebration, she canceled a $15,000 show and flew straight to Austin. She and Kenneth sang and danced for the delighted crowd. Three months later she died of a drug overdose.

Kenneth Threadgill was a living representation of the unification of Austin's past and present. He went on to appear with Willie Nelson on the album and soundtrack of *Honeysuckle Rose.* Threadgill sang "Coming Back to Texas" and "Singing the Yodeling Blues." He was paid $3,000 for acting in the movie of the same title, and $4,000 for the songs. In 1981 he released Kenneth Threadgill and the Velvet Cowpasture's first album, titled *Long-Haired Daddy.*

In 1976 his beloved Mildred died, and Kenneth sold the tavern a few years later to Eddie Wilson, who was one of those Wednesday-night regulars back in the Janis days. Wilson christened it Threadgill's Restaurant, and it features his own excellent Southern cooking.

Kenneth Threadgill died of a pulmonary embolism on March 20, 1987, at Brackenridge Hospital in Austin.

EDDIE WILSON also heads another Austin Legend. The Armadillo World Headquarters sprang from the fevered brain of Wilson, and it changed Austin forever. The Armadillo was a Petri dish for what Austin was to become. Physically it was one of the many live-music venues that popped up in Austin during the early 1970s. Culturally it was unique. The Armadillo was a hip oasis in a desert of the Easy Rider Texas attitude "let's shoot the hippies off of their motorcycles." It wasn't long before the hipness of the Armadillo spilled out into the rest of the city. Austin became a place where Cowboy and Hippie merged. Long hair and cowboy hats were unheard of in Texas in those days. The Armadillo gave those types a safe place to hang out, and in turn, Austin embraced them. A new counterculture was born.

But it wasn't only the music that made the Armadillo what it was to become. A new breed of artists began painting posters and walls and stage sets and anything or anyone that didn't move as fast as their crazed, psychedelic, often brilliant ideas. Jim Franklin was the one who transformed the image of the shy, humble armadillo (previously thought of only as roadkill) into a mystical icon that took Austin to a new level of cultural and spiritual renown. Along with Franklin, the pantheon of great artists that created and, in a sense, were created by the Armadillo includes Michael Priest, Guy Juke, and Ken Featherstone.

When Willie Nelson started playing the venue in the early seventies, he kicked off what became known as the

"Outlaw Movement." Willie and other cosmic cowboys like Waylon Jennings, Doug Sahm, Michael Murphy, Billy Joe Shaver, Steve Fromholtz, Ray Wylie Hubbard, and Jerry Jeff Walker led the charge. The Armadillo provided a home for this renaissance. Without the Armadillo as the base for these fledgling bands, no one would ever have heard of the Outlaw Movement. On the West Coast, the Byrds and The Band were creating the same kind of musical fusion, but they called it country-rock, or Southern rock. The rest of the world was unaware of Austin until Willie exploded into the national consciousness with "Blue Eyes Cryin' in the Rain."

Ten minutes later everyone wanted to come to Austin to have their hip cards punched. The best place to punch it was at the converted National Guard armory known as the Armadillo World Headquarters, where there were no seats, no air conditioning, and no pretense. The Armadillo lasted ten years. On December 31, 1980, it held its last New Year's Eve blowout, then the doors closed forever and the people went away. The building was demolished without fanfare.

Currently, Eddie Wilson's new Threadgill's World Headquarters at Riverside and Barton Springs Road sits next door to the site of the old Armadillo World Headquarters and serves as host to memorabilia from Austin's Armadillo days. Eddie calls his Threadgill's World Headquarters a "link between the new Austin and its past. In matters of music and food, we represent a time before disco or microwaves."

Eddie still owns the original Threadgill's Restaurant, located at 6416 North Lamar. This restaurant houses their banquet facility, corporate offices, and a large kitchen for catering. They are open 365 days a year, so you can't miss it no matter when you visit Austin. Eddie did a good job in creating and maintaining these living memorials to the birthplace of the cosmic cowboy movement and Austin the way I remember it. Do the Kinkster a favor and thank him for me when you see him. Then you can tennis-shoe the bill.

# A Night Out in Austin Quiz

1. For a night out on the town, do you:
   a. spend hours primping before going out?
   b. spend ten minutes primping before going out?
   c. What the hell does "primping" mean?

2. At a bar you're more likely to order:
   a. a Cosmopolitan
   b. a diet hemlock
   c. a Lonestar, baby!

3. You are:
   a. a computer geek with a chip on your shoulder
   b. a waiter at a leprosarium for unwed mothers
   c. a vampire on the nod

4. In your CD player right now you have:
   a. Sade
   b. Eminem
   c. Bastard Sons of Johnny Cash

5. At Starbucks you order:
   a. a latte
   b. another gentleman to move his fat ass
   c. Fuck Starbucks!

6. You drive:
   a. an Audi
   b. a red, white, and blue Hummer
   c. a nail through your forehead

7. When it comes to sports, you're into:
   a. miniature golf
   b. dwarf tossing
   c. ultimate Frisbee

8. If you adopted a dog, it would be:
   a. a hairless Chihuahua with a tattoo of Pinochet

b. a pit bull with your balls in its mouth
c. a stray with the eyes of Jesus

9. You name your dog:
   a. Bullet
   b. Checkers
   c. Huevos Grande

10. You smoke:
    a. Nothing! Tobacco smells disgusting!
    b. wheelchair weed
    c. somebody's pole

11. The last concert you saw was:
    a. Pat Green
    b. Yanni
    c. the Dixie Chicks in London

## Kinky's Extrapolations:

**If you answered mostly a's:** For a night out on the town, you'll have the best time in the swanky "Warehouse District." This is the place for young professionals and others who dress to impress and like to pretend they're in L.A. Check out Halycon or Trulucks, both on 4th Street. Of course they have valet parking.

**If you answered mostly b's:** Head down to Sixth Street and welcome to wonderland. With too many bars to name and constant drink specials, you'll have no problem getting "your drink on." Cheers, The Ritz, and The Bayou are all popular places frequented by the twenty- and thirty-somethings. Also have a drink or two at Flamingo Cantina, Joe's Generic Bar, and Sake on 6th, and, at gunpoint, the Hard Rock Café.

**If you answered mostly c's:** The Red River District has your name written all over it. Everyone in these bars knows who Hank Williams, the Ramones, and the White Stripes are. A few places I'd send you to would be the Red Eyed Fly, Love Joy's, Room 710, Stubbs, and Club deVille. The Red River District is located off Red River and Ninth Street, a short walk from the busy Sixth Street.

# Eat This

AFTER A NIGHT OF FESTIVITIES A LITTLE FOOD IS necessary so you don't wake up feeling like there's a small Aryan child playing an accordion in your head. One of my favorite all-night diners is the Magnolia Café. There are two locations, one on Congress and one on Lake Austin Boulevard. I like to get a giant stack of gingerbread pancakes made of whole wheat, cornmeal, and pecans. Wash it down with a shooter of homemade unsweetened lemonade. Fear not the dreadlocked, tattooed, pierced waitstaff, for their service is excellent and their conversation is often amusing. Feel free to light up a cigarette if you smoke, because Magnolia is one of the few restaurants you can smoke in without some asshole trying to make a citizen's arrest.

Another all-night diner is Kerbey Lane Café, which has four locations. In Austin you're either a Kerbey person or a Magnolia person, but you might as well hit both to figure out what kind of Austinite you'd be when you grow up. Kerbey Lane features locally grown, pesticide-free vegetables, free-range beef and pork, great entrées, and sometimes unusual fare done that way on purpose. The café welcomes vegetarians, carnivores, herbivores, and boring-vores who sit around with their cell phones and lattes, complaining that in California you can order a hummingbird-dick sandwich, so why not in Texas? Kerbey Lane is a haven for tolerance, however, so everyone is welcome. The menu covers every meal of the day; be sure to read the descriptions of the choices while you have the menu in front of you. That experience is almost as filling as the food.

Another all-night diner, and one of my favorites for tribal reasons, is Katz's Deli & Bar, located on West Sixth Street. In my opinion it's the only outlet for great Jew-food. I like to order the lox and eggs. You can also choose from sandwiches as big as your head and omelets the size of Anna Nicole Smith's nay-nays. Katz's kosher-style menu (rabbinically certified hot dogs and turkey ham are a few of the items), also include martinis, fried pickles, and stuffed jalapeños. There is a smoking section and a full bar. Katz's is an around-the-clock diner, and as the owner, Marc Katz, likes to say, "Katz's Never Kloses!" If you happen to come by any weekend night after the bars close, you are likely to meet some very interesting folks stumbling in. Last week I met a guy named Marlo who claimed he was a leg model for Victoria's Secret. He was a friendly guy who decided to just sit down at my table and engage in conversation with my party. It was quite an experience, but at Katz's you're likely to meet anyone. I did not, however, give him spare change for a sex change.

Another Austin establishment is Amy's Ice Creams. Amy's motto is "Life is uncertain . . . eat dessert first." If you're craving ice cream at midnight, or earlier, Amy's is definitely the place to go. If the server drops your order as he flips it behind his back, you get it for free—and not the one that fell on the floor, either!

Directly across the street and down a few shops from Katz's is Hut's Hamburgers. This old-fashioned burger joint has been slapping its patties long before Fuddruckers was a gleam in its corporate mother's eye. If beef burgers are not to your taste, Hut's will replace it with buffalo meat, chicken breast, or a veggie burger. Order an old-fashioned vanilla Coke and a basket of fries or onion rings to complete the experience. President Bush rates this place as his favorite burger joint in Austin.

If you find yourself getting a little puckish, Barton Springs Road is home to some of the coolest restaurants in town. This little strip of street just down the way from the park is like a miniature Waikiki where you're more likely to get stuck in foot traffic than in car traffic.

All the cafés on Barton Springs Road are excellent. They include Chuy's, "Home of Big as Yo Face Burritos and Texas Martinis." The busy décor is an ADD sufferer's worst nightmare next to standardized testing in a sixth-grade cafeteria on pizza day; don't forget to take your Ritalin! Baby Acapulco's, or Baby A's, as we natives call it, is another one of my favorite Mexican cantinas. They have great margaritas, especially the purple ones, and tasty avocado enchiladas.

Shady Grove, next to Baby A's, is about as laid-back as you can get. Outdoor seating is abundant and the Hippie Burger, a veggie patty, is my favorite thing to order. Inside they have shuffleboard to keep you entertained while waiting for your food. It'll put you into a coma in about three seconds. Lunches here are hectic as hell, so expect to be put on a waiting list. During the summer months there's live music featuring some of Austin's biggest names.

Across the street from Shady Grove is the hippest coffeehouse in Austin, Flipnotic's Coffee Space. This is a unique hangout spot, frequented by the young, the middle-aged, and some old fucks, too. Its outdoor patio makes you feel as though you're sitting in a friend's back-yard, and that's because in many ways you are. Flipnotic's design is like a 1950s outer-space movie set, and there's also a TV fish tank you can stare at for hours. Some people stare at it for their entire lives.

Here the regulars are interesting, the employees are as friendly as a golden retriever puppy, and the atmosphere is ultra-relaxed. If you aren't in the mood for a coffee, you can grab a smoothie, a beer, or even a waitress. The Chewbacca Chicken Sandwich is what I usually get. While you're there, enjoy the people-watching opportunities; the patrons are quintessential Austin. Look around and you are sure to see an elderly guy with a foot-long braided beard, a hippie girl with a homemade skirt, a computer geek who bears an uncanny resemblance to Richard Speck, a tattooed biker, and an employee with a red afro the size of a basketball, all sitting together at one table getting along and having a good time. They also play good music like Waylon and Willie, the Flatlanders, Tish Hinojosa, and basically anything that doesn't get on the Kinkster's nerves.

THE NIGHT HAWK. For me, it is redolent of the dreams of youth and the smoke of life. In the early sixties I would sit with my college friends at the Night Hawk on the Drag, or the Plantation Restaurant or Uncle Van's Pancake House, now long-dead places of business and enlightenment that exist only as smoky little rooms of the soul, where we drank endless cups of blue coffee and solved the problems of the world as we knew it. And I think at times that we knew the world better than perhaps we know it now. So the Night Hawk to me symbolizes youth as well as age, that decidedly human process of being old enough to realize, young enough to know.

Like a rare and endangered species, the Night Hawk Restaurants once numbered four in Austin. Now there is but one left, at the corner of Burnet Road and Koenig Lane. Harry Akin, a former song-and-dance man, actor, and later mayor of Austin, founded the little chain and made it a chain before chains were a bad word. Now that the chain is gone, only the jewel survives. It is called the Frisco Shop, after a famous hamburger served by the Night Hawk since its inception in 1932. The Frisco Shop itself was established in 1953.

Akin was bugled to Jesus in 1976, but his slogan lives on: "There's Nothing Accidental About Quality."

Many of Akin's former employees live on as well. More than ten of the Frisco staff have been with the Night Hawk organization for over twenty years. Many of the customers have been loyal patrons far longer than that, which is one reason I like the place so much. The demographics are great. No matter how old you may feel, you'll always find people older than you at the Frisco. This is good because the only other place with the same demographic is the Shalom Retirement Village.

Harry Akin, indeed, was somewhat of a pioneer in civil rights. In the early sixties, he and the Night Hawk restaurants led the way in integrating Austin's public dining facilities. He believed in the strange concept of judging people on their merits, and he was an equal-opportunity employer from very early on.

Last, and probably most important of all, during the later years of his life the Frisco was my father's favorite restaurant in the world. The food he always found delicious, the service excellent. The waitresses all loved Tom. They reminded me vaguely of the maids at the Chelsea Hotel in New York—so friendly and zealous they made it difficult for you to commit suicide.

I came into the Frisco a few days after Tom had lost a year-long battle to cancer. When I left, one of the waitresses ran out after me into the parking lot with tears in her eyes. She had just heard the news that Tom was dead. She couldn't believe it. I couldn't, either. I'm not sure what her name was. Tom knew all their names.

So I go to the Night Hawk whenever I can. It's a bit of a walk down Yesterday Street. And I believe that if Texas were ever destroyed in a terrorist nuclear attack, three things would be sure to survive. In San Antonio, there'd be the Alamo. In Dallas, there'd be Tom Landry's hat. In Austin, there'd be the Night Hawk on Burnet Road.

## THE KINKSTER'S TOP TWELVE AUSTIN RESTAURANTS

(Subject to change at any moment because of my fickle nature and drastic mood swings.)

Most of the restaurants (and people) I liked in Austin went belly-up about twenty-five years ago, but here are twelve places where you can't possibly go wrong. I list them, to paraphrase my father, in a random and haphazard order.

1. HILL'S CAFÉ. Bob Cole's re-creation of what was once a great restaurant and is now even better. Great food, great music, great old Austin ambiance. Best big hairy steaks in town. (South Congress Avenue)

2. THE TEXICALLI. Owned and operated by the unsinkable Danny Roy Young, unofficial mayor of South Austin. Killer-bee hamburgers, jukebox, and vintage Austin art (Check out Guy Juke's poster of John McCall's '56 Chevy. It's on the ceiling.) Don't leave without trying the Dr. Pepper Milkshake. (East Oltorf)

3. CISCO'S. Rudy Cisnero's old place, serving the best Mexican breakfasts in Austin. Note the pic of me and Willie on your way to the dumper. (East Sixth Street)

4. SAM'S BARBECUE. There are more terrific barbecue places in Austin than crossties on a railroad or stars in the sky, but Sam's brisket is the best in the world. (2000 East 12th Street)

5. THREADGILL'S RESTAURANT. Previously extolled, but worth mentioning again. A must for out-of-state visitors who want to get their hip cards punched. Try the fried green tomatoes. (Riverside Drive)

6. **LAS MANITAS.** The place to have breakfast with Austin's social, cultural, and political elite. To paraphrase my father, it's always a successful excursion when you see someone more important than you. A great photo of Austin favorite James McMurtry hangs over the counter. (Congress Avenue at Third)

7. **TOP NOTCH.** Tom Friedman's favorite hamburger place. Mine, too. (Burnet Road)

8. **TIEN HONG.** Best Chinese restaurant in Austin. Try dim sum on Saturdays and Sundays. *Dim sum,* by the way, means "to touch the heart lightly." (Burnet Road near 183)

9. **EL PATIO.** Been there forever, and it's still right up there at the top. In the fifties, before he made it big, Elvis took my friend Kara's mother here on a date. He drove her to the restaurant in a lavender Cadillac. When they walked into the place, they had to pass by a table full of frat daddies. "Hey, look!" somebody shouted. "It's Fats Domino." (Guadalupe and 29th Street)

10. **NIGHT HAWK FRISCO SHOP.** Everything I said about it is true. Believe what I tell you. Mandatory. (Burnet Road at Koenig)

11. **KATZ'S DELI.** Like I said, the best Jew-food in town.

Not to be missed at any hour of the day or night. (Sixth Street)

12. JOVITA'S. Eat killer-bee enchiladas, and on Thursday nights see and hear one of the finest country bands in the world, the Cornell Hurd Band. (South First Street)

# *Famous Austinites*

## WILLIE NELSON

$I$N THE INTRODUCTION TO THIS GUIDEBOOK, I WROTE, "In Austin they say when you die, you go to Willie Nelson's house." Well, good news, folks. You don't necessarily have to croak in order to go to Willie's place. Trust me, there are easier ways. Let's say you're a German tourist or a rising young urologist from Teaneck, New Jersey. You've heard good things about Austin, and you're down here for your first visit. You love Willie, but you've never met him. With all of the phases and stages of his life and lifestyle, how can you be sure when you meet him that it's really Willie? That one's easy. He looks like Jesus Christ on a bad-hair day.

How to find Willie's place? Well, I can't wrap your lunch in a roadmap for you, but it's on the outskirts of town. Follow Highway 71. It's called Briarcliff. Everybody knows where it is. If you get lost, you can ask the guy standing by the side of the road with the sign that says, "Need Fuel for Learjet."

You won't find Willie in any house, though; he'll either be playing golf or in his bus. If he's in his bus, it could pose a problem. He has three buses. One's for Willie, one's for the band, and one's for carrying all of the weed necessary to keep everybody on the road again. But that's not why Willie smokes dope. He told me why once. He does it to keep down the rage.

And be careful if you try to talk politics with Willie. He's a conspiracy theorist of the first water. Once, just before the war with Iraq, I was arguing with him on the bus. I was very much in favor of the war. He was very much against it. He was also smoking a joint the size of a large kosher salami. In an attempt to reason with him, I said, "Look, Willie, the guy's a tyrannical bully and we've got to take him out." "No," said Willie. "He's our president and we've got to stand by him."

But the place you're most likely to find Willie during the daylight hours (or possibly at night, wearing a miner's helmet with a headlamp) is on the golf course.

Willie owns his golf course, which makes it very convenient for him to play about forty-seven hours a day when he's not performing or helping me solve the problems of the world from inside the bus. You can play golf on Willie's course, and that, in fact, is a good way of running into him. Sometimes, however, this plan doesn't work out so well. Willie told me a story about a woman who'd recently come off his course complaining she'd been stung by a bee. The golf pro asked her, "Where'd it sting you?" She said, "Between the first and second holes." The pro said, "Well, I can tell you right now, your stance is too wide."

One of the things I love most about Willie is that, once you manage to locate him, he'll take the time to stop what he's doing (within reason) and talk to you like you're the only person in the world. That's why we call him the Hillbilly Dalai Lama. One of the most memorable things I've ever witnessed a star of any magnitude do was the time when, with the naked eye, I observed Willie Nelson standing outside his bus for three hours after a concert, signing autographs in the rain. It's what we call "dancin' with who brung you."

## JERRY JEFF WALKER

### THE WANDERER

With the possible exception of a few early serial killers, Jerry Jeff Walker was one of the first people in America to pioneer and popularize the three-word name. I've often maintained that if Susan Walker, Jerry Jeff's wife/manager (emphasis on slash), had married me instead of him, I'd be the president of the United States and he would be sleeping under a bridge. While this may not be entirely true, it is accurate to say that Jerry Jeff would no doubt be very happy sleeping under a bridge. Especially if you let him have his guitar.

Jerry Jeff is not only a Texas music icon, he's something even more important to me: a friend. When I needed help in my 1986 campaign for justice of the peace in Kerrville, Jerry Jeff was there. When the Utopia Animal Rescue Ranch held its first "bonefit," in 1999, Jerry Jeff was our headliner. I've called upon Jerry Jeff so often, in fact, that Susan once asked him, "Doesn't Kinky know any other celebrities?" I do, but few of them are as generous with their time. That's why I was happy to comply several years ago when he asked me to give him a blurb for his autobiography, *Gypsy Songman*. Now that I'm writing this chapter on famous Austinites and digging deeper into Jerry Jeff's life, I find myself in that most ironic of karmic circumstances: having to actually read a book I've given a blurb for. And you know something? It's pretty damn good.

Way back when doctors drove Buicks, Jerry Jeff rode his thumb out of his hometown in upstate New York, stopped by Key West long enough to invent Jimmy Buffett, then drifted over to New Orleans, where he sang for pennies on streetcorners. Perhaps he was curious to discover, in the words of Bob Dylan, "Who's gonna throw that minstrel boy a coin?" Jerry Jeff remembers a time when a group of fraternity boys about his own age came by and started getting on his case. "Why don't you get a job?" one of them said. "You can't just wander around with that old guitar forever." "Watch me," said Jerry Jeff.

In the mid-sixties, before he was nothing, as we used to say in Nashville, Jerry Jeff was singing in Austin. Today we would probably call him a homeless person with a guitar. During this period he wrote "Mr. Bojangles," a song that now resides comfortably among the most recorded songs of all time. Looking back, it is hard to believe that a record executive once passed on the song, remarking at the time, "Nobody wants to hear a song about an old drunk nigger and a dead dog."

"Mr. Bojangles was actually white," Jerry Jeff told me recently. "If he'd been black, I never would've met him. The prison was segregated."

"It's a perfect song," I said. "But you keep changing the melody and fooling with the phrasing. Why?"

"To discourage people from singing along."

I asked Jerry Jeff to tell me about writing "Mr. Bojangles." This is what he said: "I'd been reading a lot of Dylan Thomas, and I was really into the concept of internal rhyme. I just had my guitar, a yellow pad, and the memories of guys I'd met in drunk tanks and on the street—one gentle old man in particular. The rest of the country was listening to the Beatles, and I was writing a six-eight waltz about an old man and hope. It was a love song.

"During the time I was writing 'Mr. Bojangles,' I used to go down to the Austin city pound about every two weeks and adopt a dog. I didn't really live anywhere myself, so the dog would often stay with me awhile and then it would run away. Maybe find somebody else. At least I felt I was giving him a second chance."

Jerry Jeff got a second chance himself when he married Susan, in 1974. She is largely credited with turning his life around and turning his career into a financial pleasure. Not only does he have houses in Austin, New Orleans, and Belize, but also, quite possibly for the first time in a lifetime of rambling, a sense of home. Jerry Jeff and Susan have two children, Jessie Jane and Django, who is starting to make a name for himself in the music world. Django has an album out and a hit song, "Texas on My Mind," that was recorded by Pat Green and Cory Morrow. The Walkers credit Django's attending Paul McCartney's Liverpool Institute for the Performing Arts with honing his skills as a songwriter and performer. They are currently in the final planning stages of opening a similar school in Austin. It will be, Susan says, a nonprofit organization of international scope, teaching music as well as the music business to anyone with the talent to gain admission.

The school could someday provide young people from around the world with the kind of education, direction, and support that Jerry Jeff himself never had. His education and inspiration were often provided by the real-life characters he met on the street and on the road; he returned the favor by immortalizing many of them in his songs. Through the music of Jerry Jeff Walker, people like Hondo Crouch, Charlie Dunn, and the ubiquitous Mr.

Bojangles seem to live forever. This is important, because people today don't often get the chance to meet such men in the halls and the malls of our modern-day world.

At a television taping in November 2003, Jerry Jeff performed a few of these classics and then some songs by other songwriters. He played "The Cape," a song by Guy Clark about a kid who thinks he can fly. I've always found this song a trifle treacly, but that night it brought a tear to my eye. Then he played Ian Tyson's "Navajo Rug," which brought another tear, and Steve Fromholtz's "Singin' the Dinosaur Blues," which really started the waterworks. When "Redneck Mother," by Ray Wylie Hubbard, also put a tear in my eye, I realized that I was fairly heavily monstered.

Later, out on the street, I suddenly felt stone-cold sober. The ability to deliver another man's song faithfully is a rare enough talent, but Jerry Jeff Walker does not merely make a song his own. His magic is that he gives it to you.

## ODE TO BILLY JOE

If Carl Sandburg had come from Waco, his name would have been Billy Joe Shaver. Back in the late sixties, when Christ was a cowboy, I first met Billy Joe in Nashville. We were both songwriters, and we once stayed up for six nights and it felt like a week. Today he's arguably the finest poet and songwriter this state has ever produced.

If you doubt my opinion, you could ask Willie Nelson or wait until you get to hillbilly heaven to ask Townes Van Zandt. They are the other folks in the equation, but they might not give you a straight answer. Willie, for instance, tends to speak only in lyrics. Just last week I was with an attractive young woman, and I said to Willie, "I'm not sure who's taller, but her ass is six inches higher than mine." He responded, "My ass is higher than both of your asses." Be that as it may, you'll rarely see Willie perform without singing Billy Joe's classic "I Been to Georgia on a Fast Train," which contains the line "I'd just like to mention that my grandma's old-age pension is the reason why I'm standin' here today." Like everything else about Billy Joe, that line is the literal truth. He is an achingly honest storyteller in a world that prefers to hear something else.

Thanks to his grandma's pension, Billy Joe survived grinding poverty as a child in Corsicana. "*'Course* I cana!" was his motto then, but after his grandma conked, he moved to Waco, where he built a résumé that would've made Jack London mildly petulant. He worked as a cowboy, a roughneck, a cotton picker, a chicken plucker, and a millworker. (He lost three fingers at that last job when he was twenty-two, and later wrote one of his greatest songs, which begins with these lines: " 'Three fingers' whiskey pleasures the drinker / Movin' does more than the drinkin' for me.' ")

I believe that every culture gets what it deserves. Ours

deserves Rush Limbaugh and Dr. Laura and Garth Brooks (whom I like to refer to as the anti-Hank). But when the meaningless mainstream is forgotten, people will still remember those who struggled with success: van Gogh and Mozart, who were buried in paupers' graves; Hank, who died in the back of a Cadillac; and Anne Frank, who had no grave at all. I think there may be room in that shining motel of immortality for Billy Joe's timeless works, beautiful beyond words and music, written by a gypsy guitarist with three fingers missing. Last February, Billy Joe and I teamed up again to play a series of shows with Little Jewford, Jesse "Guitar" Taylor, "Sweet" Mary Hattersley, and my Lebanese friend Jimmie "Ratso" Silman. (Ratso and I have long considered ourselves to be the last true hope for peace in the Middle East.) Pieces were missing, however. God had sent a hat trick of grief to Billy Joe in a year that even Job would have thrown back. His mother, Victory, and his beloved wife, Brenda, stepped on a rainbow, and on New Year's Eve, 2000, his son, Eddy, a sweet and talented guitarist, joined them. Hank and Townes also had gone to Jesus in the cosmic window of the New Year.

I watched Billy Joe playing with pain, the big man engendering, perhaps not so strangely, an almost Judy Garland–like rapport with the audience. He played "Ol' Five and Dimers Like Me" (which Dylan recorded), "You Asked Me To" (which Elvis recorded), and "Honky Tonk Heroes" (which Waylon recorded). He also played one of my favorites, which, well, Billy Joe recorded: "If I could I would be tradin' all this fatback for the lean / When Jesus was our savior and cotton was our king."

Seeing Billy Joe perform that night reminded me of a benefit we'd played in Kerrville several years before. Friends had asked me to help them save the old Arcadia Theatre, and I called upon Billy Joe. Toward the end of his set, however, a rather uncomfortable moment occurred when he told the crowd, "There's one man I'd like to thank at this time." I, of course, began making my way to the stage. "That man is the reason I'm here tonight," he said.

I confidently walked in front of the whole crowd, preparing to leap onstage when he mentioned my name. "That man," said Billy Joe, "is Jesus Christ."

Much chagrined, I walked back to my seat as the audience aimed their laughter at me like the Taliban militia shooting down a Buddha. It was quite a social embarrassment for the Kinkster. But I'll get over it.

So will Billy Joe.

## BAND OF BROTHERS

A happy childhood, I've always believed, is the worst possible preparation for life. Be that as it may, my dream as a child was to grow up to be a country music star. But if you dream of becoming a country music star as a kid, you'll invariably wind up a best-selling novelist. It's just a little trick God plays on us, like the channel swimmer drowning in the bathtub. But for me, becoming a writer has been a rather fortuitous turn of events. For one thing, I've always wanted a lifestyle that didn't require my presence. For another, I've always been somewhat ambivalent about performing, and lately I've come to realize that anyone who uses the word "ambivalent" should never have been a country singer in the first place. As Joseph Heller once observed, "Nothing succeeds as planned."

With country music still in my head after I graduated from the University of Texas, I joined the Peace Corps and worked for eleven cents an hour in the jungles of Borneo. As an agricultural extension worker, my job was to help people who'd been farming successfully for more than two thousand years to improve their agricultural methods. I was supposed to distribute seeds downriver, but the Peace Corps never sent me any. Eventually I was forced to distribute my own seed downriver, which had some rather unpleasant repercussions. Still, it was in Borneo that I wrote some of my first country songs and dreamed up the great notion of putting together a band called Kinky Friedman and the Texas Jewboys.

Several years later the Texas Jewboys became a reality, a country band with a social conscience, a demented love child of Lenny Bruce and Bob Wills. The group included four Texans: Jeff "Little Jewford" Shelby, Kenny "Snakebite" Jacobs, Thomas William "Wichita" Culpepper, and myself, Richard Kinky "Big Dick" Friedman. All of us except for Wichita were Jewish. The other original members—Billy Swan, Willie Fong Young, and Rainbow Colors—were all Texans and Jews by inspiration. There were other Texas Jewboys over the years, of course: my brother, Roger Friedman; Dylan "Clitorious" Ferrero; Cowboy Jack Slaughter; Bryan "Skycap" Adams; Panama Red; Major Boles; Van Dyke Parks; Lee Roy Parnell; Roscoe West; and Arnold "Big Jewford" Shelby, Little Jewford's elder brother, to name just a few.

In 1972 we got our first big break, when Chet Flippo wrote a story about us in *Rolling Stone*. The title of the piece was "Band of Unknowns Fails to Emerge." The following year we *did* emerge, traveling about the country, irritating many of our fellow Americans. With songs like "They Ain't Makin' Jews Like Jesus Anymore" and "Proud to Be an A-hole from El Paso," we were not destined to be embraced by Mr. and Mrs. Back Porch. In fact, in 1973 the Texas Jewboys received death threats in Nacogdoches, got bomb threats in New York, and required a police escort to escape radical feminists at the University of Buffalo.

We also had an audience with Bob Dylan after a show in L.A. (he was barefoot and dressed in white robes), walked on our knuckles after hanging out with Ken Kesey in San Francisco, played a farewell gig for Abbie Hoffman in New York before he went underground (we were co-billed with a video of Abbie's recent vasectomy), and were unceremoniously tossed off the stage by the management of a Dallas nightclub and resurrected the same night at

Willie Nelson's house. On June 2 of that year, I had the rare distinction of being introduced by Hank Snow's son, the Reverend Jimmy Snow, as "the first full-blooded Jew ever to appear on the Grand Ole Opry." Through it all, the Jewboys believed that the purpose of art was not merely to reflect a culture, but to subvert it. We also believed, just as passionately, that some things were too important to be taken seriously.

What happened to the Texas Jewboys? We live in the fine dust of the far horizon, beyond time and geography, where music and dreams play in perfect harmony. Little Jewford and I still occasionally travel the world (he plays keyboards and the most irritating instrument in the musical kingdom, the kazoo). Snakebite Jacobs blows his horn with the New Orleans Nightcrawlers. The last time I saw Wichita, who played guitar, mandolin, and fiddle, he was living in his car with his dog, Dwight. Like Mr. Bojangles's dog, Dwight died—from a rattlesnake bite in a trailer park. I would like to find Wichita. Billy Swan wrote "Lover, Please" and "I Can Help" and still lives and makes music in Nashville. Skycap has a band in St. Louis. My brother, Roger, who originally managed the band, is now a psychologist with three kids and lives in Maryland. Dylan Ferrero, our tour manager, who always wore dark shades and a python-skin jacket, now teaches Special Ed in Comfort and is married to a woman named Sage, who has forty-one tattoos, signs for the deaf, and runs my website.

As for me . . . well, I am the future governor of Texas, of course. Since I first announced my intention to seek office, I have been asked where in the hell did I get the idea? It's a long story. It begins with a man named George W. Bush.

AT THE WHITE HOUSE RECENTLY, as I was advising the president on Iraq, I thought I heard him mention putting me in charge of the National Park Service. It's about time he appointed a real cowboy, I said to myself as I adjusted my fanny pack. I knew, of course, that this would not be a Cabinet-level appointment. I would probably have a portfolio of some kind, a small staff of busy little bureaucrats to do all the work, and I'd no doubt carry the title of undersecretary. That was fine with me. I'd probably be spending most of my time under my secretary anyway.

As I left the East Wing, I became more and more certain that, if not exactly offering me a position, the president was subtly encouraging me to get back into politics. I'd been on hiatus since my unsuccessful campaign for justice of the peace in Kerrville in 1986, but that was then and this was now. I remembered a letter he'd written me soon after he got elected. He thanked me for mentioning his name in one of my columns "without using any curse words," and he asked me if I intended to run for JP again. On a cold day in Jerusalem, I'd told him. Now, after practically getting vetted by the leader of the free world himself, I found myself standing ready to serve. I waited in the full-crouch position for a call from someone in the administration. When it didn't come, I couldn't decide whether to kill myself or get a haircut.

There must be a place in politics for a man of my talents, I thought. Dogcatcher might be a good place to start. I could free all the dogs and encourage them to lay some serious cable in the yards of people I didn't like. Or maybe I could run for mayor of Austin. I could fight against the fascist anti-smoking laws. I probably couldn't win without appealing to all the techno-geeks, but a good slogan would help—something like "a cigar in every mouth and a chip on every shoulder" might work. Basically, though, it'd be too small a gig for the Kinkster. I have bigger fish to fry.

Well, what about governor of Texas? That might be therapeutic, I figured. It's a notoriously easy gig, and I'd certainly be the most colorful candidate to run for the office since Pappy O'Daniel. Hell, compared with Tony Sanchez, I'm practically Mr. Charismo. I can work a room better than anyone since the late John Tower went to that great caucus in the sky. When I meet a potential voter, I'm good for precisely three minutes of superficial charm. If I stay for five minutes, I can almost see the pity in the person's eyes.

Nevertheless, being governor might be a lot of fun. I've known the last two and a half governors, and they didn't seem to be working all that hard. Of course, I saw them mostly at social events. In fact, I once mistook Rick

Perry for a wine steward at the Governor's Mansion. I said, "Hey, you look familiar. Do I know you?" And he said, "Yeah. I'm the governor, Rick Perry." Then he gave me a friendly handshake and looked at me like he was trying to establish eye contact with a unicorn. He didn't seem as funny as Ann Richards or George W., but he came off like a pretty nice guy—for an Aggie.

After some minor soul-searching, I decided to throw my ten-gallon yarmulke in the ring and form an exploratory committee headed by the dead Dutch explorer Sir Wilhelm Rumphumper. The committee had one meeting and came back with the consensus that, as long as Willie Nelson or Pat Green didn't decide to run, I could be the next governor. They offered the opinion that many of Pat's people were probably too young to vote and that Willie, God bless him, did not quite present as clean-cut an image as I did. Also, neither of them had had any previous experience in politics. Not only had I run for JP, but I'd also been chairman of the Gay Texans for Phil Gramm committee.

Though the report was encouraging, I had to admit that I was beginning to find the prospect of the governorship rather limiting. I aspired to inspire before I expired. There had to be something I could do for my country besides flying five American flags from my pickup truck and telling the guy with four American flags on his pickup truck, "Go back to Afghanistan, you communist bastard!" But what of the president's offer? To clear the boards for my race for governor, I asked my old Austin High pal Billy Gammon to check the status of my appointment. Billy's so close to the president he gets to fly in the White House helicopter. "I stand ready to serve!" I told Billy.

"I'll get back to you," he said.

And he did. He told me that while the Bushes obviously considered the Kinkster a dear friend, the president had only been engaging in light banter when he'd raised the possibility of my moving into public housing. Billy also said that though I might have made a "fantastic contribution to government," George W. could see how I might well have been a "scandal waiting to happen."

"That's good news," I told Billy, "because I'm running for governor and I'd like you to be my campaign manager."

"I'll get back to you," he said.

I got over my disappointment quickly. Like most of us, I determined that I'd rather be a large part of the problem than a small part of the solution. Besides, I've got Big Mo on my side. I'm not sure how traveling with a large homosexual will go down with the voters, but hell, I'll try anything. Just this morning, for instance, I tried making a campaign pitch to my fellow passengers on a crowded elevator. After several of them threatened to call 911, however, it unfortunately put me a little off-message. "Now that I have you people all together," I told them, "I can't remember what I wanted you for."

## O. HENRY: WILLIAM SYDNEY PORTER

### THE ROLLING STONE OF AUSTIN

Austin's unique music and independent film scene gave the city the nickname "The Third Coast." Ex-con and famous writer William Sydney Porter, better known as O. Henry, christened Austin "The City of the Violet Crown," a nickname that is still used today. The tag first appeared in a political humor story titled "Tictocq: The Great French Detective, in Austin." The short story originally appeared in O. Henry's locally published newspaper *The Rolling Stone* on October 27, 1894. The phrase is used in chapter 2: "The drawing-rooms of one of the most magnificent private residences in Austin are a blaze of lights. Carriages line the streets in front, and from gate to doorway is spread a velvet carpet, on which the delicate feet of the guests may tread. The occasion is the entrée into society of one of the fairest buds in the City of the Violet Crown."

William Sydney Porter was born in North Carolina and came to Austin in 1884. He held such varied jobs as clerk, bookkeeper, draftsman, and bank teller. He also acted in local theatrical productions. In 1894 he began publishing the aforementioned weekly newspaper, *The Rolling Stone.* He also drank heavily and often missed deadlines due to his inebriated state.

Porter fled to the Honduras following embezzlement charges by his former bank employer. He returned to Austin in 1897 to be with his wife, who was fatally ill, but was promptly arrested and sent to prison for three years. It was during his incarceration in the penitentiary that he began writing short stories under the pseudonym O. Henry (according to some sources, he acquired the pseudonym from a warden called Orrin Henry). His purpose for writing was to earn money to support his daughter Margaret. After he was released from prison, Porter moved to New York City, where he began to write prolifically (ten collections and more than six hundred short stories during his lifetime). He also began to drink prolifically. O. Henry's last years were dogged by alcoholism, ill health, and financial problems. He rose to literary fame in nine short years, but died an alcoholic at age forty-eight in a New York hospital. At the time of his death, he had twenty-three cents in his pockets. Now that's a guy after the Kinkster's own heart.

Porter's former Austin residence now houses the O. Henry Museum. He lived in this 1886 Queen Anne–style cottage from 1893 to 1895. The home, at 409 East Fifth Street (phone 512-472-1903), has since been restored and now contains artifacts and memorabilia from his life in Austin. Visitors are welcome.

## CHARLES WHITMAN

We like to think that everything's bigger in Texas. This, of course, includes mass murder sprees. I graduated from the

University of Texas in Austin in 1965, majoring in a highly advanced liberal arts program known as Plan II. The program was mainly distinguished by the fact that every kid had some form or other of facial tic. The really bright ones are probably sleeping under bridges today, but then again, genius is its own reward.

Charles Whitman was not a Plan II student, but you can't have everything. He made straight A's, he was studying to be an architect, he was a former Marine sharpshooter, and he was also an Eagle Scout. To put it on a bumper sticker, he was an all-American asshole. One day, in the summer of 1966, he climbed the Texas Tower with his trusty hunting rifle and shot forty-five people. I wrote a song about him, and in just a minute I'm going to hum a few bars.

But first let's take an analytical look at why Charles climbed the tower and I wrote the song instead of the other way around, with me climbing the tower and Charlie writing the song. Because I believe it could very well have been the other way around. All of us have a little bit of Anne Frank and a little bit of Hitler deep down in our souls, and whether you live in Austin or Boston, you've got to be careful how you adjust your carburetor. I'm just saying we've got to kind of watch it because there's a little bit of Charlie in us all. It helps, of course, if you're not an Eagle Scout.

Why is this important? Well, it's probably not. Probably nothing's important. But what I was trying to say before I began hearing voices in my head is that I believe there is something in the mindset of the Eagle Scout that provides an excellent breeding ground for the future mass murderers of America. Maybe it's just that while the rest of us were desperately trying to extricate ourselves from a turbulent and troubling adolescence, the Eagle Scout was assiduously applying himself to the narrow, maddening craft of knot-tying. It's my theory that in a universe of Eagle Scouts, you'll find an extremely high proportion of psychopaths. I can't prove my theory or establish a statistical link between Eagle Scouts and mass murderers because I don't have a computer. Nor am I likely ever to have one. I think computers are the work of Satan.

Of course, I'm wary of more than just Eagle Scouts and computers. Another pet theory of mine deals with people who have the name "Wayne." I believe we should keep an eye on these folks. Most of them are up to no good. The problem, I contend, begins at birth when the father, invariably a fan of John Wayne's, blithely borrows the name for his son. The son obviously cannot live up to the John Wayne lifestyle, and this causes a deep guilt to fester in the young little booger and one day he swerves to hit a school bus. Examples of the Wayne Phenomenon are legion: John Wayne Gacy, Elmer Wayne Henley, John Wayne Nobles, Wayne Williams, Michael Wayne McGray, Christopher Wayne Lippard, Dennis

Wayne Eaton, and Wayne Nance, merry mass murderers all.

John Wayne, of course, was not from Texas, but he acted like he was. Texas has always had a lot to brag about, and one area of which we're particularly proud is the many mass murderers who were born in the Lone Star State. There's Richard Speck, who killed eight nurses in Chicago (he was a sick chicken, then he took a turn for the nurse); Charles "Tex" Watson, Charlie Manson's executive butt-boy (never trust a guy named "Tex"); and Henry Lee Lucas, who killed about 400 million people but can't remember where he buried the bodies. Occasionally, Texans get a bit overzealous and we brag about murders that aren't even our own, so to speak. *The Texas Chainsaw Massacre,* for example, is loosely based on an incident that took place in Wisconsin.

But Charles Whitman was definitely one of our boys. (Charles Whitman, Charles Watson, Charles Manson— might be something here.) Anyway, Charles Whitman was one of the world's first modern mass murderers. On the surface he was an ex-Marine, married to some kind of university sweetheart, I believe. I myself once dated the former Miss Texas 1987. I, of course, *was* Miss Texas 1967.

So one day Charlie just climbed the tower and killed all these people. As a Texas Tower guard once told me: "It'll happen to you."

## THE BALLAD OF CHARLES WHITMAN
### by Kinky Friedman

*He was sitting up there for more than an hour,*
*Way up there on the Texas Tower*
*Shooting from the twenty-seventh floor.*
*He didn't choke or slash or slit them,*
*Not our Charles Joseph Whitman*
*He won't be an architect no more.*

*Got up that morning calm and cool,*
*He picked up his guns and walked to school*
*All the while he smiled so sweetly,*
*Then he blew their minds completely,*
*They'd never seen an Eagle Scout so cruel.*

*Now won't you think for the shame and degradation*
*For the school's administration*
*He put on such a bold and brassy show.*
*The Chancellor said: "It's adolescent,*
*And of course it's most unpleasant*
*But I got to admit it was a lovely way to go."*

CHORUS:
*There was a rumor about a tumor*
*Nestled at the base of his brain.*
*He was sitting up there with his .36 Magnum,*

## The Great Psychedelic Armadillo Picnic

*Laughing wildly as he bagged 'em.*
*Who are we to say the boy's insane?*
*Now Charlie was awful disappointed,*
*Else he thought he was anointed*
*To do a deed so lowdown and so mean.*
*The students looked up from their classes,*
*Had to stop and rub their glasses,*
*Who'd believe he'd once been a Marine?*

*Now Charlie made the honor roll with ease,*
*Most all of his grades were A's and B's.*
*A real rip-snorting trigger-squeezer,*
*Charlie proved a big crowd-pleaser*
*Though he had been known to make a couple C's.*

*Some were dying, some were weeping,*
*Some were studying, some were sleeping,*
*Some were shouting "Texas Number 1!"*
*Some were running, some were falling,*
*Some were screaming, some were balling,*
*Some thought the revolution had begun.*

*The doctors tore his poor brain down,*
*But not a snitch of illness could be found.*
*Most folks couldn't figure just-a why he did it*
*And them that could would not admit it*
*There's still a lot of Eagle Scouts around.*

CHORUS:
*There was a rumor about a tumor*
*Nestled at the base of his brain.*
*He was sitting up there with his .36 Magnum,*
*Laughing wildly as he bagged 'em.*
*Who are we to say the boy's in—*
*Who are we to say the boy's in—*
*Who are we to say the boy's insane?*

Although this chapter is about famous Austinites past and present, I would like to amend the category at the last moment because not all Austinites destined to be famous have achieved their fame yet. Some are merely en route, like this troop of Girl Scouts I met in Austin.

THE FIRST TIME I went to a charity car wash, Richard Nixon was president. I think some high school cheerleaders were trying to raise money to go to a cheerleading camp in Fat Chance, Arkansas. My vehicle was a dusty green 1953 Plymouth Cranbrook convertible with a wolf-whistle and a Bermuda bell. I was hoping to have an overnight with a few of the cheerleaders myself. Of course, that never happened. Nixon would not have approved. Besides, I was a late-blooming serious.

There were a great many things back then, no doubt, of which Nixon and society in general would not have approved. But life was different in those days—or maybe it was exactly the same, only we didn't know it. It seemed, for instance, that none of my high school friends came from broken homes. Divorce was almost unheard of. Nobody knew what a single person was. And, certainly, no one I knew had a parent in prison. I don't really think I was sheltered. I just think I was out to lunch. The second charity car wash of my life was held recently in the parking lot of the Hotel San José in Austin. I was driving a silver 1999 Cadillac DeVille that had once belonged to my father and had the distinction of being one of the few Cadillacs in Texas with a Darwin fish emblem. The vehicles had changed, and I had changed—the last thing in the world I was interested in was a fifty-eight-year-old cheerleader. The game had changed too, in this tale of two car washes. Whether we like it or not, at some indefinable point in time, we all forsake our childhood games and become players in the game of life.

The girls at the second car wash were not high school cheerleaders. For one thing, most of them weren't old enough to be in high school. For another, in their brief lives, there hadn't been a hell of a lot to cheer about. Girl Scout cookie season was over for this particular troop. So were a few other things, like home, family, and childhood. That's because every girl in this troop has or has had a mother in prison. They are Troop 1500, otherwise known as the Enterprising Girl Scouts Beyond Bars, the Austin chapter of a national program that has served more than forty-five girls with incarcerated parents since its inception in 1998.

And they *are* enterprising. The car wash was a success, with the girls washing, soaping, and spraying fifteen cars, one bike, themselves, and several customers. And many of the girls are looking confidently to the future. One bright, witty thirteen-year-old, who was raped by an uncle while her mother was in prison for running a drug ring, reads at least one book a week, and when she grows up she wants to be a librarian. A fifteen-year-old whose mother is serving time for a gang-related murder wants to be a marine biologist. A fourteen-year-old whose mother, a heroin addict, stole and forged checks wants to be a social worker; judging by how devotedly she helps the younger girls, she may be well on her way. Then there's the pretty twelve-year-old whose mother is serving fifty years for murder. This girl's stated goals are to be a horseback-riding instructor and to work with the seals at Schlitterbahn. (There are, to my knowledge, no seals at Schlitterbahn. They may have them, of course, by the time her mother gets out.) And then there's the most soulful little nine-year-old in the world. She wears beautiful braids and has never been able to live with her mother, who's in for the usual things—prostitution, theft, and using and selling heroin and crack cocaine. And the kid? When she grows up, she wants to be a veterinarian.

Are any of them going to get there? You might be surprised. According to Julia Cuba, the program executive of the Lone Star Council, which oversees Girl Scout troops in eighteen counties in Texas and Oklahoma, 96 percent of the girls in Troop 1500 have stayed in school. Ninety-nine percent have avoided teen pregnancy. Ninety-eight percent have kept out of trouble with the legal system. These are remarkable numbers, especially considering that girls whose mothers are in prison are six times as likely as other high-risk groups to end up in prison.

In the United States there are approximately thirty Girl Scouts Beyond Bars programs, most of them limited to providing only one service: once-a-month visits to the prisons. The Austin chapter, led by Cuba and regularly evaluated by Darlene Grant of the School of Social Work at the University of Texas at Austin, differs from the others in that it concerns itself with a girl's family, school, and social life and helps guide her mother's reentry into the free world. The program has been so successful, in fact, that the girls are the focus of an upcoming PBS documentary by award-winning filmmakers Ellen Spiro and Karen Bernstein (the girls are filming part of the documentary themselves).

After I dried off from the car wash, I went out to dinner with the girls. They are a smart, free-spirited, fun-loving bunch of kids. I'd never met them before, and from what I know of life, our paths may never cross again. I've always found it interesting how most of us seem to place our energies and efforts behind only those causes that directly affect our own lives or those of our families. In other words, there are better things to do on a beautiful Saturday afternoon than drive a van full of kids out to Gatesville. I was reminded of a lady I once met whose only grandchild had died. She told me, "I used to say, 'This is my grandson, and those are other people's kids.' Now I say, 'Every child is my grandchild.' "

So why did I allow myself to get soaked to the bone at a Girl Scout car wash in the first place? Just lucky, I guess. And lucky is the right word for it. Most of us were born lucky. Lucky to have a home and a family. Lucky to have someone to provide hills to climb and stars to reach for. Lucky, when we fell, to have a catcher waiting in the rye. The girls at the car wash, of course, have known precious little of those things. Outside of Julia and Darlene, all they really have is each other. Maybe it will be enough. I certainly hope so. As we like to say in rock and roll, the kids are all right.

# The Great Outdoors

$B$Y NOW YOU'VE DONE THE NIGHT LIFE, HAD SOME chow, maybe spotted a few famous Austinites. You're probably ready to take in Austin's great outdoors. Well, hop onto my pet beer belly and let me show you what's out there.

First stop is a 351-acre Austin favorite, Zilker Park, located at 2100 Barton Springs Road. Zilker (as it is called by the locals), was named in honor of Andrew Jackson Zilker, who bet on the classic American dream and hit a jackpot. When he was only eighteen, he moved from Indiana to Austin with a mere fifty cents to his name. His first night in town, he got a job washing dishes. Soon after, he got a job constructing the Congress Avenue Bridge and made friends with the owner of an ice plant who later hired him. Ol' Andrew didn't let any grass grow under his feet. During this time he was a volunteer fireman, director of the First National Bank, Water and Light commissioner, and head of the Travis County School Board. It wasn't long before he became the engineer of the ice plant, and in 1901 he began buying land between the Colorado River and Barton Creek. He acquired 350 acres surrounding Barton Springs and used the land to pasture the livestock that pulled his ice wagons.

Zilker deeded thirty-five acres around Barton Springs to the city of Austin in 1918, with the provision that the land be used for education. During the First World War, a military school was established on the grounds. In 1932 he agreed to give the military an additional 330 acres if the city would buy the acreage from the school for $200,000. The purchase was approved in a bond election, and despite the economic depression of the 1930s, the land was developed into Zilker Park. Present-day Zilker Park is the jumping-off point for so many of Austin's outdoor activities that it is hard to decide where to start. I would suggest starting at Barton Springs Pool.

Located at 2101 Barton Springs Road within Zilker Park, Barton Springs Pool has been used by people living here since Christ was a cowboy; measuring three acres in size and fed from three underground springs, it is also the largest natural swimming pool in the United States within an urban area (a bit of trivia: Robert Redford learned to swim at Barton Springs Pool when he was five years old while visiting his mother's relative in Austin).

Barton Springs Pool (also simply called "Barton Springs" by the locals) got its name from an early Texas settler named William Barton. "Uncle Billy," as he was known, built his cabin on a tract of land that included three springs. This area became known as "the Bartons." He named the three springs after his daughters, Parthenia, Eliza, and Zenobia. The largest spring (Parthenia) is now the main spring that feeds Barton Springs Pool. Eliza Springs issues from a cavelike sinkhole on the north bank near the lower end of the pool; Zenobia Springs flows above the shallow end. Some parts of the pool are colder than others (perhaps where the ghosts of drowned swimmers lurk—I worked as a lifeguard here). The warmest part of the pool is in the shallow end where a legion of little children practice synchronized urination.

No description of Barton Springs Pool would be complete without mentioning the endangered Barton Springs salamander. In 1998 the U.S. Fish and Wildlife Service named the Barton Springs salamander an endangered species, causing the lungless, red-gilled creature to become the center of a political controversy that divided the city. The controversy is far too complicated to nutshell in a few paragraphs without leaving something out, but the gist of it is that the endangered salamander, found only in Barton Springs, requires certain environmental protections that some say affect the quality of water in the Barton Springs Pool. Because the pool cannot be cleaned as often as it used to be cleaned, thick clouds of blue-green algae known as oscillatoria have overrun the waters like Gentiles on a ham sandwich. My friend Turk Pipkin, the co-editor of a 1993 book (I highly recommend) titled *Barton Springs Eternal: The Soul of a City,* expressed to the *Austin Chronicle* his dismay at the condition of the pool. "I don't think the water in the pool is as clean as it used to be," said Pipkin. "Also, men follow me with erections and pull on my ponytail. I used to feel it was a soul-cleansing experience. I don't have that feeling anymore."

Visitors can judge for themselves, but keep in mind that the Barton Springs Pool is one of Austin's famous landmarks and easily the most popular swimming hole in the city.

After splashing down at Barton Springs, you can take a long walk around the greenbelt. There is always a soccer game going on across the street at Zilker Park, and if that's not to your fancy, you can spend hours walking through the Zilker Botanical Gardens, which includes the Taniguchi Oriental Garden and the Austin Area Garden Center. The thirty-one-acre Botanical Gardens are located at 2220 Barton Springs Road, and are free to the public. In season, the butterflies are plentiful and the air hangs thick with many natural fragrances, one of which emanates from my free-range cigars.

On the other side of the Barton Springs Pool fence line is what I like to call "Dog Heaven." Here, dogs are able to run and swim freely, splash around with their ostensibly human companions, and enjoy the cold water on a hot day. If you go there enough, you'll recognize the regulars, like a carefree boxer named Waylon and a rather strange three-headed dog named Cerberus.

Near Dog Heaven is a kayak–and–canoe–rental shack. Get one of either and paddle out toward Town Lake; this is the best way to see this part of Austin. Of *course* I haven't done it yet.

Town Lake was created by the damming of the Colorado River on the west by Tom Miller Dam and on the east by Longhorn Dam. Its banks are festooned with trails that meander for miles throughout the city of Austin. People can run and bike for free on these trials, which is why I never go there (I have a fear of Lycra and windshorts). Canoe rentals are available at businesses along some parts of the trail, and the lake is especially popular with crew teams.

The Congress Avenue Bridge is in downtown Austin, just ten blocks south of the State Capitol building. The bridge spans Town Lake at the cross streets of Cesar Chavez to the north and Barton Springs Road on the south. I have exactly one fond memory of the bridge, also called the Congress Avenue Bat Bridge.

Keep in mind that fond memories are not my strong suit; anyone who knows me knows better than to reminisce about any experience, fuzzy or otherwise, we have shared in the past. Unfortunately, people insist upon reminiscing, so to better fit into society and get people the fuck off my back, I pay my friend and former Texas Jewboy road manager Dylan Ferrero to be my font of fond memories.

Dylan is ready to deploy anywhere in the world at a moment's notice, should someone want to reminisce fondly about anything we may have done or shared in the past. Dylan is good at his job, too. He can recall with clinical detail the time, place, and weather conditions of any fond memory I am supposed to have had, even though he may not have been there himself.

I have a very low fondness tolerance, owing to a rare genetic defect known as Low Fondness Tolerance, or LFT. I lack the gene for sentimentality and endearment toward precocious children. I wear a med-alert bracelet that says so. I believe my LFT originated in a long-dead relative who was fond of absolutely nothing, past memories, children, and still-life art in particular. But as I said, I do have one fond memory of the Congress Avenue bats that has defied my genetic disorder.

Many years ago my friend Jack Slaughter frequented the hike-and-bike trail at Town Lake. I happened to be staying in a hotel with an unobstructed view of the bridge so I called Cowboy Jack, one of the original Jewboys, to come up to the room to watch the bats after his daily jog. Jack had more degrees than a thermometer, and in his gentle, scholarly way he had studied the bats for years and often, at his own secret hiding place, watched them emerge from the bridge. Rather than waste the perfect room with a view on my bat-indifferent ass, I decided to share my window view with Jack (which turned out to be one of the best spots to view the bastards, and the bats, too).

Jack arrived at my room shortly after his jog; as he did during the days on the road with the Jewboys, he carried a chicken box from HEB (Herbert E. Butt, Texas's biggest supermarket chain) with his clothes and other bare essentials packed into it. Jack was a simple man, and everything he ever needed fit into those chicken boxes. Perfectly.

The bats trickled out from under the bridge exactly on cue. "Mexican free-tail bats" was all Jack said as we watched them emerge, indifferent to the *Homo erectus* crowd gathered at designated bat-watching spots around the bridge. We watched as bats began to pour out from the Congress Avenue bridge, first a small number, then, minutes later, a tsunami of flying mammals that darkened the sky.

"Did you know," said Cowboy Jack, "that Confederate soldiers mined the bat guano for saltpeter, which was used in making gunpowder? In fact, a gunpowder factory was established near San Antonio."

"No shit?" I said.

Thinking back on it, Jack was what Austin is all about. An expert on forest preservation and endangered animals, he was a gentle spirit who always reminded me a bit of Johnny Appleseed. In 2000, while jogging on the walkway of the Lamar Street Bridge, he was killed by an SUV driven by a teenager. He died almost to the moment that the bats began spiraling out from under the nearby Congress Avenue Bridge.

Of all Jack's accomplishments, and there were many, the obituary in the *Austin American-Statesman* began with "Road manager for the Texas Jewboys." That's not a bad thing, I remember thinking at the time, to have done in your life.

On the right, as you head South on Lamar across the bridge, you can see the flowers that someone still places there. The bats arrive at the bridge in mid-March and return to Mexico in early November. While in residence, they can be observed during their emergence display at dusk. Time of year, weather conditions, and colony size all affect bat emergence times. Late July through mid-August is the best time to see the impressive flights, as newborn pups first begin to forage with their mothers. The bats generally emerge before dark, but may fly late if conditions aren't favorable. For updates and approximate emergence times, call the Bat Hot Line at 512-416-5700 (category 3636).

## HIPPIE HOLLOW: LEGAL SKINNY-DIPPING

Hippie Hollow is a clothing-optional park that has gained fame as being the premier skinny-dipping spot in Texas. In the 1980s, Travis County officially took over management of this area on Lake Travis and gave it the respectful moniker "McGregor/Hippie Hollow County Park."

The county added Hippie Hollow to the county park system and made improvements such as public restrooms with water fountain, a paved access trail, stairways, trash removal, recycling bins, a paved parking lot with controlled entry, signs indicating that clothing is optional, and periodic patrols by park rangers.

A small fee will get you into the nudist "colony." Once inside, Hippie Hollow is a safe place to enjoy Lake Travis sans the confines of Gap wind shorts and Hilfiger polo shirts. The ledges are rocky, but there are many flat surfaces to accommodate lawn chairs, beach towels, and/or hands. There are several secluded coves available, but keep in mind that Hippie Hollow is a legitimate nude beach, so no public hosing!

Snack services are provided by a commercial vendor, but because the trailer is close to the main entrance at the top of the stairs, visitors must dress just enough to be legal in order to partake of this service. Just enough to be legal isn't too hard to interpret. Basically it means cover up certain areas of the body that might offend the genital police.

The park is open year-round. The hours are 9:00 a.m. to 9:00 p.m. The park closes in the summer as early as 6:00 p.m. in the cooler months. There is an eight-dollar-a-day parking fee or three-dollar fee for walk-in visitors. No overnight camping is allowed. No glass containers, pets, or open fires are permitted in the park. No pool. No pets. Ain't got no cigarettes.

To reach Hippie Hollow, from Austin, take FM 2222 approximately five miles west of Capital of Texas Highway (loop 360) to FM 620. Turn left on 620 and drive to the next signal, at Comanche Trail. Take a right onto Comanche Trail and continue for 2.5 miles. Hippie Hollow is on the left. So, what are you waiting for? It's time to strip and even out those tan lines!

# Austin Landmarks

## THE UNIVERSITY OF TEXAS

THE UNIVERSITY OF TEXAS AT AUSTIN (ALSO known by the locals as "UT" or simply "Texas") has influenced the flavor of Austin so completely that it would be impossible to imagine our city without it. As for giving you a comprehensive view of the university, its past, its present, its future . . . well, that would be more detail than the Kinkster signed on for. The short version of UT is the best I can do without killing myself by jumping through a ceiling fan.

UT, the flagship campus of the University of Texas system, is the largest public university in Texas. Established in 1883, the university is consistently ranked as one of the top public schools in the nation. It has a student population of around fifty thousand and a faculty of 2,700. Among the faculty are winners of the Nobel Prize, the Pulitzer Prize, the National Medal of Science, and the

National Medal of Technology, as well as numerous members of prestigious scholarly organizations. UT offers many notable academic programs, among them Physics, Latin American Studies, Computer Science, Engineering, Business, Law, and Astronomy (which administrates the McDonald Observatory in the Davis Mountains of West Texas). The university's doctoral programs in Botany, Linguistics, and Spanish ranked in the nation's top five. My own father was a professor here, and several of my personalities are alumni.

The university has been the driving force behind the growth of the film industry in Austin. The University of Texas Film Institute counts among its alumni Matthew McConaughey, WB president of entertainment Jordan Levin, and co-president of Sony Pictures Classics Michael Barker. The Advisory Board includes director Richard Linklater *(Slacker, Dazed and Confused)* and Jack Valenti, president and CEO of the Motion Picture Association of America.

Distinguished alumni in other fields are many. Walter Cronkite graduated from here, as did Lady Bird Johnson, Bill Moyers, William F. Buckley Sr., and Liz Carpenter.

The university's colors are burnt orange and white, and its official song is "The Eyes of Texas." The mascot is a Texas longhorn named Bevo. The original Bevo made his debut in 1916; the Silver Spurs, a men's honorary organization, handle the animal. Longhorn steers are loaned to

UT with the understanding that they will be retired after a reasonable period of time.

The sports teams are called the Longhorns, or just the 'Horns. Fans of the 'Horns are known for the "hook 'em, horns" hand sign, created by head cheerleader Harley Clark in 1955. It is made by making a fist, then holding up the index and pinky finger of your hand. Holding the hand above your head and screaming "HOOK 'EM, HORNS!" is optional. The Longhorns compete in the Big 12 Conference of the NCAA's Division I-A, and their stadium is called "Darrell K. Royal Texas Memorial Stadium" (Royal was a highly respected coach at UT).

One of the university's most visible attributes is the twenty-seven-story Main Building, or Tower, located in the middle of campus. When a Longhorn team wins an NCAA Championship, the tower is lit completely orange with the numeral 1 displayed on each side. If you live in Austin long enough, you eventually find yourself unconsciously checking the skyline for the Tower to see what color it is, even if you don't care. The Tower's observation deck was closed for the second time in 1974 after a suicide jumper used it as a launching pad to pancake himself on the courtyard below. If you have read this far, you already know about the first time the tower was closed: after Eagle Scout Charles Whitman's last stand on August 1, 1966. Well, I have good news for you, pilgrims! On September 15, 1999, the UT Tower Observation Deck was reopened. The deck offers a grand view of the UT campus and the Austin area in all directions.

Observation deck tours are available by reservation only through the Texas Union Information Center. For information on availability and the schedule of tour reservations, call toll-free 877-475-6633. Tours may be canceled owing to weather conditions and when the nation's terrorism alert status is at Orange or higher. The UT Tower is located with the Main Building, east of Guadalupe and south of 24th Street.

In conclusion, UT has done pretty well for a place that got its start as a small campus on forty acres with one building, eight teachers, two departments, and 221 students. We should all do so well.


## CHILDREN IN TREES

I'd like to tell you a little story about a big tree. No, wait. Let me tell you about the children.

No. Hold the weddin'. Let's take them both together. Children in trees. What I know about children in trees I learned from Slim, an old black man who wore a Rainbow Bread cap, drank endless cans of warm Jax beer, and listened faithfully to the hapless Houston Astros on the radio when he'd finished washing dishes on the ranch in the evening in the summertime in a faraway kingdom known as the fifties. Slim had three cats and they were continually getting into the nurse's garbage cans. This was a summer camp, you understand, with a lot of children and a lot of trees, and at the end of the summer the children would all leave but the trees would stay. They had too many leaves to leave. Anyway, the nurse once asked Slim why his cats were always going into her garbage cans, and Slim replied, "They wants to see the world."

In the final stages of alcoholism in the dead of the winter in the white man's world of the Texas Hill Country, Slim began imagining that he was seeing children in trees. Maybe there *were* children in trees. Who are we to judge? As Austin politico Ben Barnes once commented as he found himself embroiled in a giant real-estate development scandal, "Let he without stock cast the first stone."

I was seven years old at the time, but I knew Hank Williams was dead, as my little brother and I rode up beautiful, glittering Congress Avenue in the backseat of a green 1953 Plymouth Cranbrook convertible driven by my dad with my mom next to him, both so much younger than I am now. I'm fifty-eight, but I read at the sixty-year-old level.

As I remember it, my dad drove us all over Austin that night. The car, the city, and the world were new and there were many wonderful sights to see. We drove past the pristine beauty of Barton Springs and saw the moonlight glinting off the waters. We drove up to the top of Mount Bonnell and watched the twinkling lights of the sleepy city below. And finally we stopped the car and got out and my brother and I ran around under the canopy of what was the biggest tree we'd ever seen in our lives, the Treaty Oak.

"According to legend, this tree was so named," Dad told us, "because in the early 1800s Stephen F. Austin, the father of Texas, signed a treaty with the Indians beneath the branches of this giant." He told us about how this lone survivor of a grove of fourteen trees, collectively known as the Council Oaks, was regarded as a temple of worship by the Comanches and Tonkowas long before the Anglos invaded. Mom remembered hearing a legend about the secret potion the Indian women made from the leaves of this tree, mixing them with wild honey. They believed that if maidens drank the concoction during a full moon, their braves would come safely home from battle.

In 1989 a man with a two-inch penis tried to kill the Treaty Oak by pouring a drum of powerful herbicide at its base. He was caught and given nine years in prison. But the damage had been done. The ground was treated, neutralized, and some of the soil was replaced. Half of its majestic crown was removed, but it still went into shock and lost most of its leaves. Texas billionaire and former presidential candidate H. Ross Perot handed the city a blank check and said, "Do whatever it takes to save the Treaty Oak." With Perot's funding, experts were brought in and a massive, heroic effort was begun.

In 1997 the Treaty Oak produced its first crop of acorns since the poisoning. These were collected and germinated and, two years later, these Baby Treaty Oaks found homes all over Texas and neighboring states. People still make pilgrimages to the once-mighty oak to pay homage to this living symbol of Austin history.

To reach the Treaty Oak, drive west on Sixth Street past Lamar Boulevard, and take a left at the next traffic light, which is Baylor. The tree is on your left, between two shopping areas at 503 Baylor Street between West Fifth and Sixth Streets.

Today only about a third of the tree remains, but it's well worth seeing. It's still a beautiful tree. Maybe more beautiful. And, like the rest of us, the Treaty Oak is still hanging on.

Austin is also home to four other famous trees.

## MEMORIAL PECAN

Located west of the north entrance to the capital.

The original Memorial Pecan was planted on the Capitol grounds on May 30, 1945, in soil gathered from all 254 counties in Texas, to honor Texans who gave their lives in World War II. The wood from the original pecan tree was used to create a commemorative bench on the first level of the Capitol extension complex. Another tree was planted on September 24, 1993, to replace the original.

## HOGG PECAN

While the actual Governor James Hogg pecan trees planted at the grave of the governor no longer live, the pecan does have an interesting place in Texas, thanks to Governor Hogg.

Native to Texas, pecan trees were once so plentiful in the state that they were cut down just to harvest a single crop of pecans. More than one hundred varieties of pecans have been developed. I was once a judge at a Pecan Nut contest in Kerrville at the local mall (or, as we Kerrverts say, the "small") where I was instructed to examine, taste, and feel samples of pecans while their owners stood nervously by, clutching little nut leashes in their sweaty palms (or maybe I'm thinking of the Shih Tzu sheep-herding competition I marshaled). Apparently such pecan shows are not uncommon in these parts, where competition is fierce to produce nuts that offer superior taste, size, and texture.

Anyway, back to Governor Hogg. He requested that a pecan and a walnut be planted at his grave instead of a headstone. Hogg is reported to have said to his daughter and his lawyer as he lay dying: "Let my children plant at the head of my grave a pecan tree and at my feet an old-fashioned walnut tree; and when the trees bear, let the pecans and walnuts be given out among the plain people so they may plant them and make Texas a land of trees."

Within a day of making the request, the governor died (in 1909) and was buried in Oakwood Cemetery. His last request was honored. Two pecan trees were planted at the head of his grave and a walnut tree at its foot. In 1919 the Texas legislature declared the pecan the state tree, partly in honor of Governor Hogg's final request.

## SEIDERS OAKS

Located at Seiders Springs, now a city park along Shoal Creek, between 34th and 38th Streets, the original live oak grove was where Gideon White was killed by Indians in 1842, when Texas was still an independent nation. White's daughter Louisa Maria continued to live in the family cabin near the grove; later she married Edward Seiders and the couple settled by the area's springs, which became known as Seiders Springs. Edward Seiders saw a business enterprise in the springs that flowed from the rock face opposite the oak grove. He built a small resort and fashioned pools out of the springs for visitors to enjoy. By the 1870s, Seiders Springs became a tourist attraction. The Seiders built bathhouses and a dance pavilion to entertain guests. The guests were transported to Seiders Springs from the center of town.

Today, descendants of the original oaks are fixtures along the Shoal Creek greenbelt, where they stand in Seiders Springs Park.


## LODGINGS

The Austin Motel's red neon sign rises up like the phallus of a mighty phoenix out of the ashes of South Congress Avenue. Many a tourist has gazed in wonder at the sign ("The Austin Motel: Corporate-Free Since 1938!") before turning to the nearest person to ask, "Is that a dick? That's a dick! Gawd-*damn!*"

Welcome to my favorite stage-stop in town.

The Austin Motel is a brick-and-mortar reminder that the American dream can still happen to ordinary people through ordinary hard work. While it is true that there are no Austin Motel franchises or big-shot stockholders or multimillion-dollar profits, it is nevertheless a success story that bears testimony to sixty-six years of stubborn endurance that has survived several generations, economic downturns, vandalism, and the gradual deterioration of the once-friendly neighborhood. The motel's spirit was too big to break, however. She rallied in the early 1990s when the daughter of the second owner moved back to Austin to restore the old motor inn. Dottye Dean, along with a loyal staff, many of whom had a hand in the renovation of the motel, brought it back from the brink of death. The motel is a bit more modern today, but its spirit remains the same quaint, old-fashioned, corporate-free lodging it started out as. Fittingly, there is a statue of Don Quixote on the premises, in the rear parking lot. (The motel is located at 1220 South Congress Avenue, in the SoCo shopping district.)

ANOTHER OF THE KINKSTER's favorite lodgings is the San Jose on South Congress, practically side-by-side with the Austin Motel. Even though the two motels are near each other, they aren't rivals. They coexist more like sisters: where the Austin Motel is the solid, down-to-earth, sensible one, the San Jose is pretty, sophisticated, and chic; she attracts the trendy clientele, the Hollywood crowd, those who want the extras without the sterility of the chains. The Austin Motel is more my speed, but don't worry; if one doesn't please you, the other will. (The San Jose is located at 1316 South Congress Avenue.)

## AUSTIN'S MOONLIGHT TOWERS

In Bandera, Texas, is an establishment called the Frontier Times Museum, which features exhibits like the two-headed goat, the left shoe from an "unknown negress," and, most famous of all, the Timmy D'Spain Shrine. Timmy was a young boy who went to Jesus after he was beheaded by a wire strung across the dirt road upon which he was riding his motorbike. The shrine includes Timmy's G.I. Joe dolls, a shirt (not the one he was wearing at the time of his decapitation, much to the disappointment of generations of summer-camp children visiting the museum on field trips), and various other mementos of his short life. I never knew little Timmy, but I have visited his shrine many times whenever I got a hankering to see the left shoe of an "unknown negress."

The Austin Moonlight Towers have nothing to do with the Frontier Times Museum or Timmy D'Spain, but according to "Ripley's Believe It or Not," an eleven-year-old kid named Jimmy almost died when he fell from the 165-foot tower at Guadalupe and Ninth Street, bouncing along the sides on the way down. Unlike the unfortunate Timmy, his head remained attached. He awoke from a nine-day coma with 187 stitches to mark his fall. Of course, he won't get a shrine at the Frontier Times, but it is a bit of interesting trivia about these famed towers and Jimmy does rhyme with Timmy.

I have lived in Austin on and off for much of my life. The Moonlight Towers were never a part of my guided tours for my out-of-town friends. Actually, I never gave any out-of-town friends any guided tours, but I am speaking hypothetically, both of the tours and of the friends. I didn't really discover the Moonlight Towers until I started researching this book. Suddenly I started seeing them everywhere.

The Towers have been in almost continuous operation for over one hundred years, and have been turned off only twice. The first time was for a week in 1905, and the second time was briefly in 1973, during the national energy crisis.

The Austin Moonlight Towers were purchased by the city from Detroit in 1894. A single tower cast a bright light from its six carbon-arc lamps that illuminated an area three thousand feet in diameter. In those days, such light towers were common in cities, and were used in place of streetlights. Mercury vapor lamps are now used in these 165-foot triangular cast-iron and wrought-iron structures.

Austin is the only city in the United States that still uses this once-popular tower lighting system. The towers are listed on the National Register of Historic Places. Seventeen of the original thirty-one towers are still in use.

In 1995, during the celebration of Austin's one hundredth birthday, the city completely restored each tower and replaced them at their original sites. Most of the towers can be found in residential areas near downtown. A few remain in the downtown area. The towers are landmarks you can take your friends to see after you drive them by where all the really interesting and cool places used to be.

Where to find Austin's Moonlight Towers:

- Nueces and West 4th
- Guadalupe and West 9th
- Blanco and West 12th
- Rio Grande and West 12th
- San Antonio and West 15th
- Nueces and West 22nd
- Speedway and West 41st
- Lydia and East 1st (Cesar Chavez)
- Trinity and East 1st (Cesar Chavez)
- Trinity and East 11th
- Coleto and East 13th
- Chicon and East 19th (MLK)
- Leona and Pennsylvania
- Eastside Drive and Leland
- South 1st and West Monroe
- Canterbury and West Lynn
- Zilker Park

## HAUNTED PLACES IN AUSTIN

The most famous place to see dead people, or, using the more politically correct term, Apparition-Americans, is the city's own State Capitol.

The Capitol's oldest ghost is that of Robert Marshall Love, who was the state comptroller early into the twentieth century. He was shot on June 30th, 1903, while at his desk. W. G. Hill, a former employee of the state comptroller's department, shot him, and as Mr. Love lay dying, he said, "I have no idea why he shot me. May the Lord bless him and forgive him. I cannot say more." His body was later buried at Tehuacana, his hometown. His spirit stayed in the state capitol, where it can be encountered as it wanders the second floor of the east wing during off-hours.

Occasionally it has been reported that he appears to visitors and watches them as they tour the building. Sometimes he speaks, saying "Good day," but he disappears before a reply can be given. He has even been captured on security camera videotapes, where he is seen standing near the old Comptroller of Public Accounts office. Those who encounter the ghostly Mr. Love report that he is always very polite and well dressed in a business suit that appears to be from the early 1900s. I have never personally seen him, but that could be because I have never actually been inside the State Capitol.

THE DRISKILL HOTEL is another hangout for Austin's Apparition-Americans. It opened its door to the public on December 20, 1886, on a city block purchased by cattle baron Jesse Lincoln Driskill for $7,500. Colonel Driskill (an honorary title given him by the Confederate Army during the Civil War) paid out $400,000 to build the hotel. He hired the best designers of the time, Jasper N. Preston and Sons of Austin, to design the original cream-colored brick and limestone building. The good colonel had busts of himself and his sons, Tobe and Bud, installed around the top of each entrance.

Soon the Driskill became the premier showpiece for the frontier town of Austin, the place to be seen if you were a politician or an aspiring politician. On January 1, 1887, the Driskill hosted its first inaugural ball for newly elected Texas governor Sul Ross. In October 1898, Austin's first long-distance telephone call was placed from the lobby. Less than a hundred years later, former president Lyndon Johnson often watched election returns in the Driskill. The hotel was the headquarters for the media during Johnson's administration. Certainly, history has been made within the walls of this "frontier queen" hostelry. The Driskill has been the meeting place of legislators, lobbyists, and the social leaders of Austin, and was the site of inaugural balls, elaborate banquets, receptions, and university dances and ceremonies. Like its neighbor the State Capitol, the Driskill also has its own ghosts.

Those who have been in the presence of these ghosts say that one of them is certainly Colonel Driskill, who so loved his hotel that he never left. According to Austin Ghost Tours, Driskill announces his presence by the smell of cigar smoke. Unfortunately, this means that Colonel Driskill copped the entrance I had planned to use in my ghostly form. Now, for the sake of originality, I am limited to flatulence or other gas-emitting preambles to announce my presence to the living (or, in my continuing effort to be politically correct, Animated Americans).

An Apparition-American who co-haunts the Driskill with the colonel is the four-year-old daughter of a U.S. senator. The child haunts the grand staircase that goes down to the lobby of the hotel. The story goes that she was playing near the stairs and was killed when she slipped and fell while chasing a ball. The front desk staff has heard her bouncing the ball down the steps and laughing.

More recently, the ghost of the "Houston Bride" has appeared on the fourth floor, hurrying to room 29 in the early morning with her arms full of bags and packages. According to the Austin Ghost Tour, the living woman checked into that room in the early 1990s. Her fiancé had unexpectedly called off their marriage, which left the spurned bride inconsolable. Once settled into her room, she decided that a shopping spree, courtesy of her ex-fiancé's credit cards, would be just the thing to make her feel better. Three days later, concerned hotel staff investigated her room because she had not been seen since she breezed out of the fourth-floor elevator with her arms filled with bags and packages. Much to the horror of the staff, the Houston Bride was found dead in the bathtub, where she had committed suicide by shooting herself in the stomach. She walks the halls of the fourth floor (but not in a long black veil). Many other ghosts have been seen in the hotel, but the Houston Bride, the ball-chasing four-year-old, and Colonel Driskill are the best known.

Currently, pre-apparitions of the Kinkster himself can be viewed quaffing a Guinness or a few shots of Jameson's, sans bullhorn, at the Driskill bar.

The Texas State Capitol visitor center can be reached at 512-305-8400; for tour information phone 512-463-0063. Visitor parking is available in the parking garage at San Jacinto and Twelfth Street.

The Driskill Hotel is at 604 Brazos Street, phone 800-252-9367 or 512-474-5911.

For Austin Ghost Tours, call the Hideout Theatre at 512-443-3688.

I will end this chapter like we end our lives—in the bone orchard. Here is a guide to Celebrity Gravesites in Austin:

AUSTIN MEMORIAL PARK
2800 Hancock Drive
Austin, TX 78731

BIBB FALK, COACH AND LAST SURVIVING MEMBER
OF THE 1920 WHITE SOX
Born: January 27, 1899
Died: June 8, 1989

JAMES A MICHENER, PROLIFIC WRITER
Born: February 3, 1907
Died: October 16, 1997

ZACHARY SCOTT, ACTOR
Born: February 24, 1914
Died: October 3, 1965

STEVIE RAY VAUGHAN MEMORIAL
Town Lake

STEVIE RAY VAUGHAN, MUSICIAN, GUITARIST
Born: October 3, 1954
Died: August 27, 1990

TEXAS STATE CEMETERY
909 Navasota Street

STEPHEN F. AUSTIN, THE FATHER OF TEXAS
Born: November 3, 1793
Died: November 27, 1836

JOHN B. CONNALLY, TEXAS GOVERNOR WOUNDED
IN THE KENNEDY ASSASSINATION
Born: February 27, 1917
Died: June 15, 1993

MIRIAM "MA" FERGUSON, FIRST WOMAN
GOVERNOR OF TEXAS AND SECOND WOMAN
GOVERNOR IN THE HISTORY OF THE UNITED STATES
(BY FIFTEEN DAYS)
Born: June 13, 1875
Died: June 25, 1961

FREDERICK BENJAMIN GIPSON, AUTHOR (WROTE
*Old Yeller* AND *Savage Sam*)
Born: February 7, 1908
Died: August 14, 1973

BARBARA JORDAN, U.S. CONGRESSWOMAN
Born: February 21, 1936
Died: January 17, 1996

# Going Native

VACATIONERS CAN USUALLY BE DIVIDED INTO TWO groups: those who want a Learning Experience and those who want to kick back and do what the locals do. I address this chapter to the latter.

What do Austinites do for fun? Where do they go to buy their books, their music, their fat-free wheat germ? What do Austinites read? What do they listen to? What do they watch? Funny you should ask because I'm fixin' to tell y'all.

Even though the average Austinite seems different from your garden-variety Texan, if you scrape away the angst and look at them carefully under a strong light, you'll find that underneath it all they aren't any different from an East Texan or a West Texan or a North Texan or a South Texan. They're all Texans, and in this state that can only mean one thing. You got a football fan on your hands, pal.

## The Great Psychedelic Armadillo Picnic

Football is as vital to a Texan as are air and water to anyone else. If our schoolchildren could read as well as they can count by sixes (TOUCHDOWN!), the educational system in Texas would rank higher than a rat's ass, which is about where we are currently. We revolve around the pigskin, make no mistake about it. On Friday nights at your neighborhood high school stadium, there will be as many as fifty thousand people in attendance to watch sixteen-to-eighteen-year-old boys living out the best moments of their lives. After graduation the shine on those golden boys starts to fade and they begin to look forward to growing a crop of boys of their own to carry on the tradition of "hit 'em again, *harder!*" In Texas, every sturdy male worth his mud flaps dreams of the day his son can take the field and get blitzed by another man's son. Hell, the only place in Texas where you can safely pat another man on the ass is the gridiron.

High school football is an animating force here in Texas, whether you want it to be or not. You might not know the difference between a quarterback and a wetback, but that doesn't matter, football will still affect you. Just try to drive anywhere on a Friday night between 9:00 and 11:00 p.m., and you'll see what I mean. Few things in life are worse then getting bogged down in the testosterone frenzy that is the post-game traffic jam. The best you can do if you find yourself in that predicament is park, let the oversized man-children thunder past, and inhale the musky scent of steroids they leave in their wake.

WHEN THEY AREN'T GOING to football games, Austinites like to celebrate with festivals, but in keeping with its penchant for the weird and eccentric, Austin usually chooses to celebrate weird and eccentric things. Spamarama is an excellent example of a festival that is uniquely Austin.

SPAMARAMA
(The Official Pandemonious Potted Pork Party)
Annual Spam Cook-off, Spamalympics, and SpamJam
www.spamarama.com

SPAMARAMA, sanctioned by Spam's manufacturer, the Hormel company, is Austin's premier bar party, where the lowly spam loaf takes center stage. The national media loves this festival. CNN first covered it in 1984, giving it international attention. The two founders of SPAMA-RAMA, Dick Terry and David Arnsberger, thought of the event in 1978 while discussing the sacred Texas tradition, the chili cook-off. Terry mused, "Anyone can cook chili. . . . Now if someone could make Spam edible, that would be a challenge. We ought to have a Spam-off." And so they did.

First held in 1980, SPAMARAMA has become one of the traditional rites of spring, like Eeyore's Birthday Party or cramming thirty people into a Kia Sportage for a drive to the coast. The Spam cook-off doesn't attract as many competitors as the ubiquitous Barbecue and Chili cook-offs around Texas, but it always did attract a broad cross-section of amateur and professional Spam-slingers from all over the country who come to Austin to compete with such dishes as Spambrosia, Jurassic Pork, and Spama-LamaDingdong (by Spam king "Chef Spam" John Meyers, who has won more SPAMARAMA cook-off trophies than anyone else in the world).

SPAMARAMA has gained a great amount of respect since its inception over twenty years ago. Famed Austin artists Jim Franklin, Micael Priest, Danny Garrett, Sam Yeates, Eddie Canada, and Guy Juke, among others, have created poster art for this porky festival. *Austin American-Statesman* humor columnist John Kelso has written about it; Austin swing band Ray Benson and Asleep at the Wheel have performed at the SpamJam, as have Alvin Crow, Flaco Jimenez, Greezy Wheels, Austin Lounge Lizards, and Ponty Bone. Past judges have included the likes of Liz Carpenter and various government officials. The Silver Anniversary of SPAMARAMA was in 2003; that year the festival was held at Waterloo Park. Even the Hormel company has begrudgingly given its official okay; it provides the official T-shirts, ball caps, and other Spam memorabilia. In an interview that Dave Arnsberger gave to the *Weekly Wire* in 2000, he told Margaret Moser, "Every year they [Hormel] try to stop me from doing something else. Last year they complained about the 'Pork Pull.' Remember when they took Jim Henson to court over the Spam character in that Muppet movie? Hormel spent days in court claiming this, that, and the other. When Henson's lawyer got up, he said they only had two words to say to Hormel: 'Lighten up.' The judge ruled in favor of Henson."

EEYORE'S BIRTHDAY PARTY
Pease District Park and Wading Pool
1100 Kingsbury Street
512-448-5160
Last Saturday in April, 11:00 a.m. until dark
Free admission

I like donkeys. I have two and a half donkeys living at my ranch in Texas (the half-donkey is a tiny menace that my friend Angel Spoons nicknamed "Bad Hee-Haw" due to its penchant for biting and kicking its herdmates. Bad Hee-Haw has since reformed and now goes by the name "Little Jewford"). I have never actually been to Eeyore's Birthday Party, but I have always liked the gloomy donkey because of a passage I read in the book when I was a child, which embodied my philosophy of life at the time. It went like this:

> "What did you say it was?" he asked.
> "Ah!" said Eeyore.
> "He's just come," explained Piglet.

## The Great Psychedelic Armadillo Picnic

*"Ah!" said Eeyore again.*
*He thought for a long time and then said: "When is he going?"*

Austin's celebration of Eeyore's Birthday Party began in 1964, when University of Texas student Lloyd W. Birdwell Jr. and his friends decided to honor the arrival of spring as they imagined Christopher Robin might have. Locals and visitors have continued this tradition every spring; the birthday party's activities include maypole dancing, a Hippie Queen pageant, beer, turkey legs, snow cones, and other fare.

Bad Hee-Haw/Little Jewford and I plan to stay at the ranch this year (as every year) because we prefer kicking and biting to maypole dancing and turkey legs. After all, in the words of our friend Eeyore, "One can't complain. I have my friends. Someone spoke to me only yesterday."

### THE TEXAS BOOK FESTIVAL

People say that us Texans have a lot of wide-open spaces between our ears, but that doesn't always apply to folks in Austin. We even have our own annual book festival here every November, started by First Librarian Laura Bush back when George W. was governor. Back then he was just thinking of running for president and I was just thinking of having another shot of Jose Cuervo Especial. Today they tell me I'm one of George's favorite writers. Of course, he's not that voracious a reader.

But that was when I first met him. At the book festival.

Authors had come from all over the world, and that night there was a big party given for us by the Bushes at the governor's mansion. I'd had a few drinks and was fairly well walking on my knuckles by the time I got there. I was dressed Texas casual, with black cowboy hat, long black preachin' coat, and brontosaurus-foreskin boots. And, of course, I was smoking a Cuban cigar. I saw Larry McMurtry's name tag in the little basket on the front portico of the governor's mansion. Obviously he hadn't shown up. So I picked up his name tag and slapped it on my preachin' coat.

Austin is widely regarded as the most progressive city in Texas, and that is not an oxymoron. The place was packed with authors, highbrow literary types, and wealthy patrons of the arts. The mansion itself was a perfect locus for this gathering of luminaries, as much of Texas's rich history is reflected upon its walls. Texas, of course, has had some pretty colorful governors, including Pappy Lee O'Daniel, who had a band called the Light Crust Doughboys. I had a band called the Texas Jewboys. Pappy Lee's campaign slogan was "Pass the biscuits, Pappy!" One of my most requested songs is "Get Your Biscuits in the Oven [and Your Buns in the Bed]." The parallels are uncanny.

You can't list colorful governors without mentioning our first and probably greatest governor, Sam Houston, who was, of course, drunk and sleeping under a bridge with the Indians when they found him and persuaded him to take the office. And then there was George W., whom I hadn't yet met.

It wasn't long before people began coming up to me and saying, "Mr. McMurtry, you have done *so* much for Texas." They were so sincere that I didn't have the heart to tell them I wasn't Larry McMurtry. So I just shook their hands and smiled and said, "Thank you kindly." Other people came over and they shook hands with me and they said, "I can't *believe* I'm shaking hands with Larry Mc*Murtry*." I smiled and said, "Thank you kindly."

As this situation progressed through the evening, I noticed George W. watching with a certain bemused interest. Finally he came over with a rather quizzical expression on his face. I explained to him that McMurtry was a shy little booger and would never be this outgoing himself, so actually I was giving him some good PR. The governor just chuckled to himself and whispered something to one of his security people. I figured I was being eighty-sixed from the function, and when that didn't happen I went over and asked the security guy what the governor had told him. The security guy looked around furtively, then told me, "The governor said, 'I want that guy for my campaign manager.'"

George W. and I have been good friends ever since.

AUSTIN, BEING THE HIGH-TECH university city it is, loves its bookstores. Yeah, we have the corporate chain bookstores here, but why patronize those places when you can go to a local store that has attitude and soul?

BookWoman
918 West 12th Street (12th and Lamar)
512-472-2785

There are almost no sure things in life; 100-percent guaranteed usually tallies out to 99.9 percent and that remaining .1 percent is often the killer. There is one sure thing I know of that I can say with 100-percent certainty, and that is this: my song "Get Your Biscuits in the Oven [and Your Buns in the Bed]" has never been played in the Book-Woman store, ever. There is not even a .1-percent chance that it has. I think the refrain "You uppity women I don't understand, / Why you gotta go and try to act like a man, / But before you make your weekly visit to the shrink, / You'd better occupy the kitchen, liberate the sink" torpedoes any chance of that happening. I am not offended that this is true. Instead, I find comfort in knowing I have contributed this small piece of certainty to an uncertain world. It brings a level of assurance during these .1-percent times.

That said, the BookWoman bookstore deserves to be supported because it contributes to Austin's unique, independent flavor. Where you spend your dollars does make a difference, so, as the BookWoman proclaims, "Go support your feminist bookstore; she supports you!"

> BOOKPEOPLE
> 603 North Lamar
> 800-853-9757

In 1970 the edge of the University of Texas was a student slum. From the wasteland of this slum, a haven for readers sprang from the cracks in the concrete like the proverbial rose in Spanish Harlem. At the time the store was called Grok Books. Grok flourished, nurtured lovingly by book lovers.

The store, which later became BookPeople, carries regional titles, as well as small-publisher titles. Their inventory-control staff resides in the store, which means the store knows its clientele and their tastes. Its mission in the world is to fight the homogeneous blight that massive chain bookstores leave in their wake. Here, you decide what you want to read, not some Book of the Month Club cult leader. It is one of the establishments that campaign actively to keep Austin weird.

REMEMBER GOOD OLD MIRABEAU and the settlement of Waterloo? Perhaps fittingly, Waterloo is now the name of what I like to think of as the best record store in the world.

And also, perhaps fittingly, it's on Lamar Street. It all makes sense now, doesn't it? Not really.

WATERLOO RECORDS AND VIDEOS
600 A North Lamar Boulevard
512-474-2500

Waterloo Records has been in Austin for over twenty years. While the store specializes in Texas Music, it has a large and diverse selection of artists from every genre and style, filed all together alphabetically, not by category. This, of course, means that Texas music star Willie Nelson and Las Vegas lounge singer Wayne Newton are filed together in the same neighborhood as Nelly the hip-hop star and boy band N'Sync. That visual experience alone is reason enough to visit Waterloo.

Waterloo Records and Videos has been voted Best Record Store in the *Austin Chronicle* readers' poll since the store's first year in 1982. It has always been a home for the music lover; it pays attention to what matters to its customers, not what matters to some random marketing strategy devised by business major interns who never see the light of day beyond their Dilbert cubicles. You can listen to any record in the store before you purchase it. If you purchase a record, take it home and play it, you still have ten days to return it for whatever reason you choose. All you have to do is bring it back with your receipt within ten days and you will get an exchange or store credit.

When was the last time you heard of a music store doing that? I will take the liberty of answering my own question. Never. Do like the Kinkster does, and go to Waterloo Records and Videos for all your music needs (speaking of yourself in the third person will only impress the salesperson).

WHEATSVILLE CO-OP
Wheatsville Grocery
3101 Guadalupe
512-478-2667

Wheatsville Co-op is owned and operated by its members. In operation since 1976, what makes Wheatsville different from any other grocery store in Austin is that it is owned and operated by people who work together to provide for themselves—in other words, its members. You become a member of the co-op; when the co-op makes a profit, it is cycled back into Wheatsville to increase services to its members, or, if enough profit is made, it is given back to the membership in the form of a patronage refund.

When Wheatsville first started in 1976, it relied completely upon the members to run the store on a volunteer basis. These days they have a paid staff who handle the day-to-day operations, but members can still volunteer. Wheatsville offers a 10-percent discount to members who volunteer, whether it be helping out in the store, working in the office, site maintenance, writing for the newsletter, or serving on the co-op committees or board of directors.

Wheatsville has a variety of membership and payment plans. If you are interested in joining, call the store or visit it at the address listed above.

AUSTIN HAS AN EXCELLENT NEWSPAPER called the *Austin American-Statesman*. In it you can find your usual city newspaper things like news, sports, classified ads, and comics. Most important, you can also find my friend John Kelso's column in the *Statesman*. He has a real eye for the city, and he hits all the humorous angles with guided-missile precision.

IF YOU WANT TO GO beyond the norm, here's a paper you should get. You can find it just about everywhere in town and it doesn't cost a cent: the *Austin Chronicle*. Still wild and free, fresh on the stands every Thursday, the *Chronicle* was voted the best news source by its own readers in 2002. The personal ads alone provide better reading material than any tabloid rag available. Austinites call Thursdays "Chronicle Day."

ON THE NEWSSTANDS, don't miss *Texas Monthly* magazine (I write a regular column that appears on the last page).

The magazine is a dead-on guide to all the people, places, and events all over Texas. It's been in business for over thirty years and has over 2 million readers. Writing for *Texas Monthly* is the first real job (other than hand) that I've ever had in my life.

## ON THE AIR

Given our obsession with music, it's not surprising we also revere our local radio stations.

### KGSR, 107.1 FM

FM 107.1, or KGSR, is a tireless supporter of local musicians, despite being a major radio station that could afford to be lazy by spinning rotations of whoever the latest tattooed, pierced, Botox-injected fifteen-year-old of the moment happens to be. By playing local artists, the station exposes their work to the listening public who, in turn, drop a dime to go to local clubs to see them perform. This benefits all areas of the local music scene. Kevin Connor is my favorite at the station, though he's on too early in the morning. (Request line: 512-390-5477.)

### KUT, 90.5 FM

KUT is a public radio station that makes its home at the University of Texas. Despite the fact that KUT airs standard NPR programming (which tends to make all public radio stations sound alike, whether they broadcast from Charlton Hestonville, California, or Earthmother, Vermont), KUT strives for variety in its program schedule by airing plenty of local programming that is uniquely Austin. John Aielli's *Eklektikos* is a good example of this. The show started in the early seventies when host Aielli was in his twenties. It is now KUT's longest-running radio show, and its programming reflects John's eclectic tastes. During any given show, listeners can hear a wide variety of selections from a deep pool of musical, literary, and theatrical sources.

Larry Monroe, who, I believe, has been at KUT even longer than John Aielli, has what I consider the most soulful late-night music show on the planet. Monroe's love of, and grasp of, virtually any music that's good is truly remarkable. And his personal CD collection may possibly be more extensive than the entire inventory at Waterloo Records. When it comes to music, Larry Monroe's emotional heritage is richer than almost anyone I know. And I'm not just saying that to get airplay. Though it couldn't hurt.

The station is one of the city's favorites, frequently ranking above commercial radio stations, according to Arbitron, the radio industry's most important collector of audience data. Because KUT is a public radio station, it is dependent upon listener contributions; in strong shows of audience loyalty, KUT regularly raises more money than public radio affiliates in Houston and Dallas, whose markets are much larger than Austin's. (Request line: 512-471-2345.)

## KLBJ-FM AND 590 AM

Would it be too obvious to state that KLBJ is owned by the Johnson (as in Lyndon B.) family? I like the AM station because it carries Rush Limbaugh and Dr. Laura. Every culture gets what it deserves.

(KLBJ AM listener call-in line: 512-836-0590. KLBJ FM request line: 800-299-KLBJ.)

## KVET-FM, 98.1

KVET-FM hosts *The Sam and Bob Morning Show,* Austin's number-one morning show. My old friend Sammy Allred teams up with Bob Cole to host the only major call-in show in America that does not employ a call screener; the result is a spontaneous, uncensored, unique platform where Austinites can dictate the topic of the moment, no matter what it is. Sam and Bob's guests are not interviewed. Instead, they sit in and participate, like the time Governor George W. Bush sang "Jingle Bells" with Larry Gatlin, or when I challenged Dwight Yoakam to reveal at what age he lost his virginity (he deftly side-stepped the subject). You never know what you're going to get when you tune in, which is a rarity in these timid times of rigidly formatted radio.

I don't know if it's because I'm growing older or going

insane, but I've become increasingly fond of Bob Cole in recent years though not in a sexual way. As for Sammy Allred, unless you're a constipated, humorless prig, he's funny enough to make you shit standing. But there's more to Sammy. He's also a philosopher, a musician, and a storyteller. He gets my vote for being the Oracle of Austin.

(KVET request line: 512-390-KVET.)

LOCAL TELEVISION EXISTS on our cable access stations, but why would you want to watch TV when you can just go to Sixth Street and see more in five minutes than you would see in an entire hour of *Queer Eye for the Straight Guy*? The only thing I will say about television is:

AUSTIN CITY LIMITS

In a nutshell, *Austin City Limits* is live music. Pure and simple. This phrase has been the motto of the show since its premiere in 1976. The show presents the best of America's music from country, blues, and folk, to rock and roll, bluegrass, and zydeco.

While the Armadillo World Headquarters was nurturing the live music scene in Austin back in the early seventies, the creators of *Austin City Limits* were taking copious notes. In the years since its inception, the show has featured more than five hundred different regional and international artists, from Willie Nelson (who headlined the first *Austin City Limits* show aired on PBS) to Roy

Orbison, Fats Domino, Lyle Lovett, Dwight Yoakam, Leonard Cohen, and John Prine. It can safely be called an Austin Institution. I did a show for them once with the Texas Jewboys, but it was never aired. Imagine that.

For those who wish to visit the studio (contrary to popular belief, the show is not filmed out of doors), KLRU's *Austin City Limits* studio doors are open to the public for official, organized tours every Friday beginning at 10:30 a.m. Admission is free. Visitors can pose on the stage in front of the famous Austin skyline backdrop and have their picture taken (bring your own camera).

*Austin City Limits* hotline for taping information: 512-475-9077. To schedule informal tours at other time, call 512-471-4811.

# Lost in Austin

*T*HIS IS THE FAVORITE TIME FOR ANY AUTHOR. IT'S called, in Truman Capote's words, "Having written." But, looking back on this little book, I can't help realizing the vast number of seminal people and magical places I have been unable to include, mostly because of space constraints and personal sloth. Texas music alone is an impossible task to chronicle faithfully. You have to dig like an archaeologist through thirteen levels of shit before you reach the lost city. When you get there, all you might find is Bob Wills's cigar next to Mance Lipscomb's guitar.

People will no doubt ejaculate: "How could you write a book about Austin without mentioning the legendary what's-his-name?" Easy, actually. This is the Austin that I know. Most of the Austin I used to know, along with most of my mind, is gone anyway, so everything comes out in the wash if you use enough Tide. As the Beatles once sang:

"There are places I'll remember / All my life though some have changed."

Some of the personality profiles in this book previously appeared in my regular column on the back page in *Texas Monthly* magazine. *Texas Monthly,* as I have mentioned, is a cultural, not to say mental, institution based in Austin, from which my editor, Evan Smith, has vowed to "fire me out of a cannon" on the day I officially announce my candidacy for governor of Texas. Hell, I don't even have a platform. If I did, they'd probably try to put a trapdoor in it. Anyway, if you do come to Austin and you see me being driven around in a long black limousine, you'll know I'm either dead or governor, both of which, in Texas, have often amounted to pretty much the same thing.

If you should run into me on the street and I'm pleasant, thoughtful, and engaging, it probably isn't me. It's probably a Kinky impersonator. There's a lot of them in Austin. Don't be fooled. If, by some fortuitous circumstance, you should run into Willie, please kiss him for the Kinkster and give him this message from me: "How can I meet you on the bus if you keep moving it?"

WILL THIS BE ON THE TEST?

## You Know You're from Austin If . . .

1. You mourn "the old Austin" even if you weren't there to experience it.
2. Your music collection contains CDs from bands no one outside South Austin has ever heard of.
3. You've eaten a hamburger at the original Hut's.
4. You're registered to vote, have firm opinions about the candidates, but have never actually cast a vote on election day.
5. You have bared buns at Hippie Hollow before they charged an entrance fee.
6. You say you're from Austin rather than from Texas.
7. You have lost sleep over the fate of the endangered Barton Springs Salamander.
8. You think Willie Nelson should be president.

## Are You New Austin or Old Austin?

If you wear a straw cowboy hat with hair down to your ass, you're old Austin.

If your white Beemer convertible has an "I love Michael Dell" bumper sticker, you're new Austin.

If you think Armadillo is the name of a city in the Panhandle, you're old Austin.

If you think that Bat Guano is the name of the Congress Avenue Bridge, you're new Austin.

If you think that Sixth Street is one big fern bar, you're old Austin.

If you think Kenny Chesney is playing tonight at the Broken Spoke, you're new Austin.

If you have an original poster by Jim Franklin, you're old Austin.

If you have a reprint of an original poster by Jim Franklin, you're new Austin.

If you remember Oak Hill as being way the hell out of town, you're old Austin.

If you think of Dripping Springs as being way the hell out of town, you're new Austin.

If you love Willie Nelson, you're both old and new Austin.

# Austin Word Search

```
Q   H   O   L   L   I   D   A   M   R   A   E   H   T   E
S   M   N   W   O   R   C   T   E   L   O   I   V   N   U
I   A   G   O   N   N   B   W   S   T   P   J   A   K   N
X   R   X   D   S   E   G   B   S   P   W   M   W   R   E
T   C   E   E   V   L   B   H   I   X   D   W   I   A   V
H   I   K   O   T   U   E   E   O   E   S   C   B   P   A
S   A   A   O   T   F   H   N   I   R   K   E   A   R   S
T   B   L   S   H   O   O   R   E   P   N   T   T   E   S
R   A   N   T   L   E   F   S   E   I   E   S   S   K   E
E   L   W   L   X   Y   N   R   E   V   L   N   L   L   R
E   L   O   P   K   Y   R   R   K   Y   B   L   D   I   G
T   W   T   N   V   Y   J   Q   Y   C   E   G   I   Z   N
D   R   I   S   K   I   L   L   H   O   T   E   L   W   O
R   K   S   A   L   A   M   A   N   D   E   R   H   K   C
R   E   V   I   R   O   D   A   R   O   L   O   C   T   D
```

| | | |
|---|---|---|
| BATS | BEVO | COLORADO RIVER |
| CONGRESS AVENUE | HIPPIE HOLLOW | SXSW |
| KINKY FRIEDMAN | KVET | LONGHORNS |
| MARCIA BALL | O HENRY | RICK PERRY |
| SALAMANDER | SIXTH STREET | STUBBS |
| THE EYES OF TEXAS | TOWN LAKE | VIOLET CROWN |
| WILLIE NELSON | ZILKER PARK | THE ARMADILLO HQ |
| DRISKILL HOTEL | | |

## Glossary

**Austin.** 1. The capital of Texas. 2. Stephen F., the father of Texas. 3. An overused name sported by bullet-headed children from Texas.

**Convict Hill.** A street that has existed in Austin since before last week.

**The Drag.** Shopping district located on Guadalupe Street from Martin Luther King Jr. Boulevard (or MLK) to 29th Street. Named for the impossible parking situation.

**Dubya.** George W. Bush. Texans like to assign a nickname to anything with a heartbeat, so it was only natural we would take a single letter, give it two syllables, and slap it on our governor.

**MoPac.** A highway, also called Loop 1. MoPac was named for the train that barrels down the center of the damn thing (Missouri-Pacific). It is thought of by many old Austinites as the Blacktop Beast, for the way it has changed the landscape of some areas. When you approach the city from Oak Hill, the sweeping, elevated, double-decker highway is usually the catalyst for such comments as "What the fuck! What *is* that? This part of town looks *nothing* like it used to! Where'd Convict Hill go?"

**Sixth Street.** The entertainment district.

**SoCo.** The South Congress Avenue area, where you can buy all kinds of shit you couldn't buy at its Yankee sister, SoHo.

**Tejas.** What Texans sometimes call their state. Texans themselves as *tejanos*. A *tejano* can also be a type of Mexican country music that features the instrument of Satan: the accordion.

**University of Texas.** Also called "Texas," or "the Longhorns." The Longhorns are the only football team you are supposed to follow; if you are caught following another team, you will be hung from the Tower and pelted with bad poetry from the university's Lit. 101 class.

## Acknowledgments

The author would like to thank the following Texans for their help and input: Sage Ferrero, Zarah Kenter, Nancy Parker, Max Swafford, and Dylan Ferrero, A/K/A Angel Spoons, P.I.

## About the Author

KINKY FRIEDMAN is the author of sixteen mysteries (published, conveniently, in sixteen different languages) and a columnist for *Texas Monthly.* He is the founder of the band Kinky Friedman and the Texas Jewboys, which, among other things, became famous for the song "Get Your Biscuits in the Oven [and Your Buns in Bed]," and for touring with Bob Dylan. The Kinkster lives with his five dogs, a pet armadillo, countless imaginary horses, and a much-used Smith-Corona typewriter on a ranch in the Texas Hill Country. With any luck, he claims, he will be the next governor of Texas.